D0718099

WITHDRAWN FROM
THE LIBRARY

KA 0045430 3

MULU
The Rain Forest

MULU

The Rain Forest

Robin Hanbury-Tenison

FOREWORD BY LORD HUNT
AFTERWORD BY LORD SHACKLETON

Weidenfeld and Nicolson
London

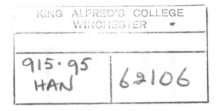

KING ALFRED'S COLLEGE
WINCHESTER

915·95
HAN

62106

First published in Great Britain by
George Weidenfeld & Nicolson Ltd
91 Clapham High Street
London SW4 7TA
1980

Copyright © Robin Hanbury-Tenison 1980

All rights reserved. No part of this publication may be
reproduced, stored in a retrieval system, or transmitted in
any form or by any means, electronic, mechanical,
photocopying, recording or otherwise, without the prior
consent of the copyright owner.

ISBN 0 297 77768 8

Printed in Great Britain by
Butler & Tanner Ltd
Frome and London

Photographs are reproduced by kind permission of the
following expedition members. S.C. Bisserot, 1, 26, 27,
29, 31, 32, 40; N. de N. Winser, 2, 3, 5, 6, 8, 9, 15, 21,
43, 44; Robin Hanbury-Tenison, 4, 7, 11, 12, 13, 14, 18,
35, 36, 37, 38, 39, 41, 42, 45; Joe Anderson, 16, 28; Philip
Leworthy, 17; A.C. Jermy, 20; Andy Eavis, 23, 24; Dave
Brook, 22; Tony Waltham, 25; Hans Friederich, 30;
Mark Collins, 33; G.P. Lewis, 34.

For all Mulu people

Contents

Illustrations

Acknowledgements

I OWE everyone concerned with the expedition more thanks than I can possibly express, both for making it all happen and for providing the information in this book. Many people and organizations are mentioned in the text or the appendices. I hope any I have left out will forgive me.

Special mention must, however, be made of the following:

The Director of Forests, Sarawak, and his staff, in particular Paul Chai, the forest botanist, whose active co-operation in this joint exercise ensured its success.

All the Malaysian Government departments which took part or assisted us: notably the Sarawak Museum, the Department of Agriculture, the Department of Irrigation and Drainage, the Sarawak Medical Service, the Royal Malay Air Force and the Departments of Customs and Immigration.

The Royal Geographical Society.

The Royal Air Force.

All our sponsors and grant-giving bodies, but especially Shell, who bore the brunt.

All the members of the expedition who checked and commented on the text, above all Clive Jermy, for whom no thanks can ever be adequate for all he did throughout.

Nigel Winser and Shane Wesley-Smith, my right and left hands before, during and after.

Rosa Mashiter, my secretary, and Barbara Preston, who typed the manuscript.

While I have made every effort to check all scientific references with those concerned, I alone am responsible for the opinions expressed and any errors of fact.

Robin Hanbury-Tenison

xi

Foreword

Lord Hunt of Llanfair Waterdine
President of the Royal Geographical Society

NEARLY 150 years ago, the Secretary of the newly founded Geographical Society of London recorded a minute of a discussion at its Council
meeting on 10 December 1831:

[Council considered] a letter from Captain Drinkwater RN recommending a Mr Coulthurst, just about to proceed to travel in Africa, to the good offices of the Council ...
Without entering into the question whether Mr Coulthurst was quite suited to conduct
such an enterprise, still, as he was going at all events, and on his own funds, it seemed
the duty of the Society to assist him so far as it easily could, in so spirited an undertaking.

During those early years in the history of the Royal Geographical Society,
the variety of choice for venturers such as Mr Coulthurst to set forth on
journeys of discovery was, to all intents and purposes, infinite. He was among
a few exceptional individuals with the means and leisure to engage in such
an enterprise. The globe, then, showed vast areas of land and ocean uncharted
other than in broadest outline and many coastlines were only crudely
sketched.

Neither the Council nor those intrepid men whom it supported in the early
1830s are likely to have cast their minds forward a century or so in time,
nor to have harboured doubts about the shape of things to come: about the
evangelistic work of missionaries in the van of Britain's war against the slave
trade and zealous to save the souls of the natives; about the rush of European
powers to carve up, colonize and exploit the resources of Africa and parts
of Asia, in order to meet the demands created by an industrial revolution;
about white hunters who would come to practise the killing of wild life, calling it 'game' in the sacred name of sport. Indeed, an illustrious former President, Sir Clements Markham, reviewing, as Secretary of the Society, the
exploration in which the RGS had been involved during its first fifty years,
felt moved to give it as his opinion that, 'Africa has been a glorious field
of generous rivalry among civilized Europeans.' Such was the spirit of those
times.

In my own early life the tempo of this era of change had passed its peak. In my teens our school atlases were already daubed with large areas in red to identify the territory of the British Empire; there were other extensive patches in different colours, to show the colonies of Germany, France, Portugal, Belgium and Holland. Some of the destructive activities of that era were still in full swing. As a child I had pored over pictures in a book about nineteenth-century explorers, which showed men engaged in a ruthless war against wild life; one sketch of a mass harpooning of whales comes vividly to mind across the span of more than fifty years. Even in the 1930s, when I served in India, it was a matter of considerable prestige to bag a record number of tigers.

Still less could those early office-bearers of the Society have foreseen other cataclysmic agents of change which also played a part in changing the face of nature: wars in the jungles, to which the late Mr Tom Harrisson, with his unique knowledge of Borneo, referred in a paper read before the Society in 1964. They could not have conceived of the emergence of new nations to replace the colonists, nor the destructive effect on primeval forests of quelling the tribal and political uprisings which followed in the wake of those take-overs. The entry of these newcomers upon the world stage has stepped up the exploitation of raw materials to meet the needs of swelling populations and the demands for ever higher standards of living. To add to all this there is now the global industry of tourism, itself a product of urbanization and the distribution of prosperity. This booming industry is becoming a significant source of income for the developing nations; but its effect may be to reduce still further the remaining wilderness and the animal kingdom within it, as well as changing the life-style and even threatening the survival of its human inhabitants.

Now, a century and a half after the early probings into Africa, the voyages to the polar regions and the great desert journeys, we are witnessing belatedly a groundswell of human misgivings concerning the affront which man has wrought against nature. For some species of life it is too late; for others the writing, were they able to read it, is on the wall. The tigers in Nepal's forests, once numbered in several thousands, are now, at the best estimate, down to a few hundreds. Happily there are still a few areas, such as north-east Greenland, where musk oxen, Arctic hares and foxes co-exist fearlessly with human visitors. Happily, too, enlightened self-interest is also at work, seeing the practical need to slow down, to plan and control extraction of minerals and felling of trees, and all other action which destroys natural countryside. There is a growing awareness, too, that the tourist trade stands to suffer from over-development and despoliation of those areas of natural beauty which are the focus of its attraction. A nascent sense of aesthetic values has been stirred. Governments are awaking to the importance of preserving the wonders of nature for their intrinsic value; and to the need to retain natural outlets for man's adventurous and questing spirit, which is no less vital to the future of the human race than those natural resources on which we depend for our material well-being.

And there is another thing. The happenings reported to us daily by the news media are causing many thinking people to question the validity of some of the beliefs and values on which our society has contrived to make such giant strides during the brief span of 150 years, and the philosophy of limitless economic expansion and self-seeking engendered by those values.

In the conservation of nature the Royal Geographical Society has a part to play. Of course it still remains essential to our *raison d'être* to promote field research and to do so increasingly in collaboration with other scientific bodies allied to the various geographical disciplines, on an international as well as on a national plane. We have, too, a vitally important duty to encourage youthful exploration, enabling the younger generation to pursue their own adventurous quests and to make their own discoveries. There can, however, be no question but that we should also join with all those who fight to save the virgin lands, to prevent pollution, to protect wild life and to husband the resources of nature for the continuing benefit of man's spiritual, quite apart from his physical, needs.

This brings me to the expedition which is the subject of this book. It was an expedition with a difference. The field work took place in a remote area of the island of Borneo, lying in the north-eastern part of the State of Sarawak, which had been designated a national park. But by accepting an invitation from the Sarawak Government to draw up a management plan for the park, the Society has undertaken a task, in line with the cause of conservation, which is novel in our history. That task, involving as it did the assembling of numerous scientists from many universities in and outside the United Kingdom for the purpose of studying the ecology of a rain forest, making an inventory of its botanical and zoological riches and studying the geomorphology of the mountainous terrain, amounted to an undertaking of mammoth proportions. It called for people with exceptional ability and qualities of leadership. The Royal Geographical Society has never lacked such people when opportunity called for an important project. In Robin Hanbury-Tenison, supported by Nigel Winser and a group of cheerful, competent and dedicated helpers, the Society fielded an ideal team for the job in hand.

With some knowledge and personal experience of other major expeditions I can say with confidence that this expedition, in terms of harmonious and effective team work, was quite outstanding. Some of its value for the future will, of course, be preserved in academic institutions which were involved in the research work. But it will depend, in a more important sense still, on the decisions to be taken by the Sarawak Government.

I will permit myself the pleasure of ending on a note of personal experience with the expedition. My wife and I spent a fortnight with Robin and his team, consorting with scientists whose knowledge was beyond our understanding, but whose enthusiasm impressed and infected us. We were fascinated by the excitement of one expert in his discovery of a host of centipedes which made a good life for themselves in the guano deposited over millennia by millions of bats in a deep, dark cave. As an enthusiastic amateur ornithologist myself, with claim to some knowledge of Indian, Himalayan and European birds, and, having been a keen collector of butterflies in Europe and Asia, I felt inadequate and frustrated by my inability to see, let alone identify most of the numerous exotic creatures in the forest. I have prided myself on being a competent navigator in thick weather and being reasonably fast and footsure on a mountain; I was clumsy and sluggish in the forest, disoriented, humbled by the speed and easy economy of movement, the intuitive sense of direction displayed by the forest-dwelling Penans and the Berawan people, by the skill of Robin himself and those who had adjusted to the conditions during more than twelve months' experience. I felt oppressed and exhausted by the sheer difficulties of travel beneath the dense, dark canopy of trees, in humid heat and torrential rain, without a vista to lift my spirits. Yet at the end of a four-day journey across those rugged mountains Robin, who had escorted us, seemed to be as spruce and fresh as before we had started out.

But despite these personal shortcomings there were many delights: those dramatic moments when a splendid panorama was revealed to us as we stood on a high ridge above a secret valley during our trek around the limestone peak of Api; when we arrived, as first-comers, on the two rocky summits of Batu Pajing; the quality of friendship which we enjoyed with everyone engaged in the work of the Gunung Mulu expedition; because of these my wife and I agreed that this had been a novel experience for us which we would not have wished to miss. I hope that, with wise and farsighted management of that rich and beautiful land, future visitors will find there the same delight in their own personal discoveries in the years ahead.

John Hunt

Part One

THE EXPEDITION

1

Conception, Gestation, Birth

THE idea of the expedition was born for me one day in June 1975. A letter arrived out of the blue, addressed to Marika and me, from Anthony Galvin, the Roman Catholic Bishop of Miri in Sarawak. In it he said that he had read our books on Indonesia and liked them; he invited us to come to Borneo so that he could show us the country and introduce us to some of the people he had come to know in almost thirty years' living there. It was a delightful letter, full of charm and good sense, and we answered it at once saying that we would try to arrange a visit in the New Year.

That same evening John Hemming, our closest friend, came to stay. He had recently taken over as the Director and Secretary of the Royal Geographical Society and he told me that a new expedition grant had just been received. It had been given by Algy Cluff, who had done part of his National Service in Sarawak and later started a successful oil company. He hoped that some of it would be used to promote exploration in Borneo and John felt that this was an area where the RGS could do useful work. Indeed, discussions along these lines had already taken place. He wondered if I had any ideas. The coincidence was too good to miss.

We duly went to Borneo on a reconnaissance early in 1976, visiting Sabah and Brunei before travelling with the bishop in the interior of Sarawak and growing to know him as one of the saintliest and yet most human and humorous of men. He convinced me of the value of a research expedition to the Baram.

We met him for the first time in Miri and went together by longboat to the headwaters of the Tinjar river. Staying in Kenyah longhouses with him was an instruction and a delight. He spoke all the local languages, interpreted and explained their customs and traditions to us, and taught us how to behave. Everywhere we were received with special hospitality because of the great affection everyone felt for him. We learned to walk carefully up the slippery notched poles from the river's edge to the raised verandahs of the longhouses; to accept a ceremonial drink of fermented rice wine on entry;

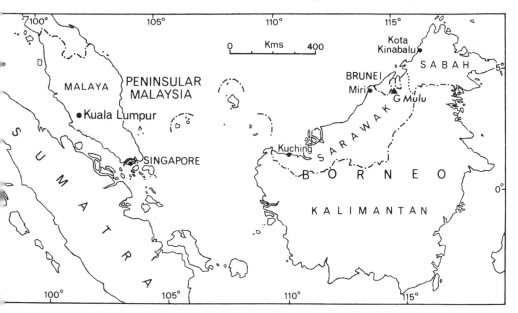

to sit cross-legged for hours on end while further drinks were pressed on us, songs sung in our honour, feasts prepared and dances performed. We learnt that we ourselves would always have to dance as well – or as badly – as we were able.

The old men who sang to us were accompanied by a chorus of attractive girls with ear-lobes stretched for seven or eight inches by heavy brass weights. Perhaps partly because of these they moved slowly and gracefully when dancing, fluidly imitating the flight of a bird, with hornbill feathers attached to their hands. The songs themselves were translated by the bishop. I later became familiar with their peculiar mixture of humble self-abasement and exaggerated flattery. They were always tempered, I felt, with a sharp humour and a deeper insight and meaning than the words themselves disclosed. In the case of the bishop, they knew him well and told at length of his goodness and wisdom, of the many long journeys he had made over the years through the jungles and rivers of their land, and of the great kindness and help he had always given them. With Marika and me they had to rely largely on imagination, but their observation was acute, their ears tuned to rumour and their comments not always as flattering as they appeared.

Behind and below us the river gurgled past in the night, the frogs and cicadas called, lamps flickered, dogs, chickens and pigs jostled for position beneath the longhouse, babies slept and children played as an old man sang:

Our house is poor and the harvest is bad. We have nothing to offer you but a few bones from an old chicken. You know the world and have seen much. You are wise like our parents, a strong tiger-man. Your wife has golden butterflies for hair. You must think us backward and stupid and we are ashamed. We can only paddle our small boats, walk on logs without falling into the mud below, and hunt the shy deer. How much more must you be able to do. Help us to learn from you so that we too may understand everything and be happy.

We continued by longboat up the Tinjar past more longhouses and beside the Dulit range of mountains where forty years before, in 1932, a previous major British expedition had taken place. It had been led by Tom Harrisson and, although I did not know it at the time, a member of that expedition, Edward Shackleton, had travelled on his own across the Baram and up the Tutoh river to make the first ascent of Gunung Mulu. Later, as Lord Shackleton, and President of the Royal Geographical Society, he was to be the patron of our expedition there. At the limit of navigation on the Nibong river, a tributary of the Tinjar, we reached a Penan longhouse. These traditionally nomadic people had settled some time before, and with government help had built themselves a beautiful longhouse roofed with shingles; they were making the change from hunting and gathering to farming. While Marika and the bishop returned downstream to visit other longhouses on other tributaries, I joined a group of young Penan men and made my way across the foothills of the Usan Apau plateau to the Belaga river.

In August 1976 the bishop came to stay with us in Cornwall and we laid the final plans, delighting in the prospect of spending much time together for we had grown very fond of each other. A week later he died in the night of a massive heart attack.

So many people in Britain and Sarawak worked to make our expedition a success that I can never hope to thank them all. But for me Bishop Galvin will always remain its progenitor.

Flying over Borneo. Green, uniform blankets of colour. Mangrove blending into forest. Rivers meandering, easily plotted from the air. A yellow fringe of sand outlining the sea, broken only by muddy estuaries. The largest equatorial island of all, third largest in the world. Dense, endless, thick with vegetation, safe, it would seem, from anything man can do to it, but with hidden wealth in scattered taller, harder, older trees, needed for furniture, floors, houses and plywood. The rest of the forest valueless but destroyed in the extraction process, and now networked with red-brown earth forestry roads. Not safe, endangered as a forest, as an ecosystem, as a habitat for innumerable creatures adapted to it. Large, beautiful animals and small strange ones. Flying lemurs, gibbons, clouded leopards, flying lizards, pit vipers, chameleons, millipedes, spiders.

The tropical rain forest is the richest environment on earth, as rich in Borneo as anywhere else, perhaps richer. It is the source of oxygen for man and other animals to breathe; it is the cause of climate, the absorber of monsoons, the engenderer of the diversity upon which life depends. It is Nature at its most alive, most varied, most energetic. Within it are more species competing to fill more niches and in the process creating, with time, yet more of each. It is an environment not only beautiful and interesting, rich and alive, but also valuable. Unchanged for tens of thousands, if not millions of years, yet it is developing all the time, with much to teach us about the world we inhabit, what we can make of it and life itself.

Now, suddenly, tropical rain forest is more interesting still because it is threatened. 'In twenty-five years it will all be gone at the present rate of timber extraction,' says the World Wildlife Fund. Understanding more about it might help to save it and all the life it holds. At the very least we would know more about what we had lost when it was gone.

And so the concept of an expedition began to take shape.

On my reconnaissance I spoke to many people, all of whom were concerned about what was happening to the forests of Borneo and welcomed the idea of urgent research. For two months Marika and I travelled in Sabah, Brunei and Sarawak. Previously we had gone deep into the heart of Kalimantan together. My brief was to assess the logistical, political and scientific implications of mounting an expedition and to recommend a suitable location for it.

The island of Borneo is larger than England, Spain and Portugal put together, or the state of Texas. It is divided between four states. Kalimantan, taking up about two thirds of the island, belongs to Indonesia; many of the least-known parts of the island lie within its borders and much fascinating research in unexplored areas waits to be undertaken. However, the political and bureaucratic difficulties of mounting a major operation in Indonesia at that time looked immense. Costs would be very high and travel into the interior would be slow and difficult.

Sabah, previously British North Borneo and now part of the Federation of Malaysia, looked much more promising and I was particularly attracted to a remote plateau called Gunung Lutong, guarded by sheer two-thousand-foot cliffs and so far unvisited by researchers in any field. I flew over the area and reached its foothills overland. The local people, Muruts, told me they never went there and supplying a base camp on the plateau itself would pose a lot of problems.

Brunei is a small independent British Protectorate between Sabah and Sarawak. It is rich from the oil produced offshore and we had many friends and contacts there including a cousin of mine who was an ADC to the Sultan of Brunei. We were able to fly over much of the state by helicopter and see the tall undisturbed forests as well as looking at a possible site for an expedition base at Sukang on the Belait river. During the same flight I glimpsed for the first time the white cliffs and towering peaks of the Mulu range across the border in Sarawak, a wild and impressive piece of country even at that distance, but I gave it no further thought at that stage.

Politically stable, geographically diverse and culturally fascinating, I had left Sarawak until last in my survey of Borneo's four states since it seemed almost too obvious as the best choice. The Usun Apau especially had much to recommend it, being very little known and undisturbed as well as being the legendary homeland of the Kenyah and Kayan people who expressed great interest in the possibility of moving back there.

It was uninhabited now except for some groups of nomadic Penan, and its name in their language means 'mountain garden'. Their legends are supported by discoveries in the 1950s of the remains of longhouses, burial grounds and traces of cultivation.

It was thought that they had been driven out some two hundred years ago by Iban headhunters and had been forced to settle on the Baram and its tributaries, in the process themselves displacing certain other tribes who already lived there. Now the growth of the timber industry was making inroads into their farming land, while a recent government survey had indicated that the Usun Apau might be suitable for agriculture. This therefore seemed a possible site to recommend for the expedition where, with government interest and the enthusiastic support of the local population, we might be able to undertake a valuable enterprise.

In Kuching, the capital of Sarawak, I had some discussions along these lines with government officials and my ideas were well received. But it was not until we reached Singapore, where I met and talked to Dr Robb Anderson, who had worked for many years with the Forest Department in Sarawak that the suggestion was first made that the expedition should be to the newly-created Gunung Mulu National Park. It had been largely through his efforts that the park had come into existence and throughout the planning, execution and aftermath of the expedition his advice and experience were invaluable. The park had only been gazetted some four months before, in December 1975, and it almost exactly fulfilled the modern concept of what a national park should be. With an area of 210 square miles it was the largest park in Sarawak and contained an extraordinary diversity of forest types and land formations. All but a small proportion of the park was virgin forest, unexploited and unoccupied except by nomadic Penan* people. The fauna, flora and land formations were said to be of exceptional scientific interest and Joseph Yong, the Director of Forests of Sarawak,† under whose jurisdiction the national park fell, had already indicated to the World Wildlife Fund that he would welcome a survey being made.

I made a quick trip to Kuala Lumpur, the capital of Malaysia, where both government and university contacts were encouraging and the British High Commission offered their full co-operation. Ken Scriven, the Director of the World Wildlife Fund of Malaysia, was particularly enthusiastic and suggested that we stood a good chance of receiving a grant from his organization. So I returned to England and delivered my report to the expeditions committee of the Royal Geographical Society. It was resolved that, if possible, an official RGS expedition to Mulu should be organized. A Mulu sub-committee was formed and I was invited to lead the expedition. None of us suspected at that stage that it would grow into the largest, longest and most productive expedition ever organized by the society.

We then wrote to Joseph Yong to ask if he would allow a team of scientists into the park to draw up, in co-operation with Malaysian scientists and government officials, a draft management plan for the park. Mr Yong replied most promptly, saying that he supported the proposal and that he had passed our request to the Chief Minister, who gave his permission for the project. Our hosts were to be the Forest Department and Paul Chai, the forest botanist, was appointed liaison officer to the expedition.

* There is some confusion about the usage of Penan and Punan – some apply either term indiscriminately. The best current usage seems to be to call Punan the similar ethnic groups, traditionally nomadic forest dwellers, but often settled. Throughout this book I have used the term Penan to refer generally to the eastern groups, who inhabit the fourth and fifth divisions of Sarawak as far as the Baram river to the west.

† At this time the position was still called Conservator of Forests. However, since it was changed to Director of Forests in order to conform with other departments in 1977 I have used the latter throughout to avoid confusion.

This was the beginning of a very close and happy relationship with the Sarawak State Government. In due course many other departments of both the State and Federal Governments became intimately involved with us, including Agriculture, Irrigation and Drainage, the Sarawak Museum, Immigration, Customs and the Armed Services. The crucial role each department played during the fifteen months we eventually spent in the field will become apparent; but I never dreamt we would receive such wholehearted and generous help from all those we had dealings with, both in and out of government, as we did in Sarawak. I know of no other country in the world where so much co-operation would be forthcoming or where so much could have been achieved with so few bureaucratic difficulties.

Meanwhile, we wrote to all the universities and scientific institutions in Malaysia inviting them to take part, liaising on the work to be undertaken between Paul Chai in Kuching and Clive Jermy our scientific co-ordinator at the British Museum (Natural History) in London. At the end of the day thirty per cent of all participants in the expedition were from Malaysia, making it, with the addition of some fifteen per cent from ten other countries, a fully international operation.

I was fortunate in having one of the most expert, interested and helpful committees that an expedition leader could wish for. The planning meetings at the RGS had a tendency to develop into animated discussions of Mulu's scientific potential, but under David Stoddart's able chairmanship the routine matters, upon which I needed advice and decisions, were always dealt with. Those members of the committee who were able to join the expedition from time to time were model guests, never expecting to be treated any differently from other members of the expedition and, without exception, leaving all of us feeling hugely encouraged that we were doing well and that the headaches were worth it.

So many expeditions in the past seem to have been marred by friction between the leader and the committee and I worried how the division of authority and responsibility inevitable in such an arrangement would work out. I need not have done so, since they were all experienced travellers who understood without being told how many problems there are in organizing the simplest operation in the field – especially in the Far East – and they simply congratulated us on our successes without dwelling on our failures.

Clive Jermy's role was vital. From the very beginning I relied on him totally in all matters scientific. It was he who vetted applications from scientists who wished to join and approached those he and the committee felt would be valuable additions. He himself made a botanical reconnaissance to Mulu in the autumn of 1976 and brought back vital information on the logistics of reaching the area and working it as well as making invaluable contacts with the scientific and governmental community in Kuching. I often felt that he should have been the leader, and I the administrative assistant, since he always knew so much more than I did about what was going on. But he was much too kind and sensitive to let me feel that the same idea might have occurred to him.

Having our home office at the RGS itself made a tremendous difference. We received patient and sympathetic back-up from the staff of the Society for the whole of the three years it took to plan, execute and wind up the expedition. In particular, John Hemming, the Director, and his assistants Jane Gordon and Deborah Boys supported us with endless letters requesting technical help and finance.

One of the first priorities for most serious expeditions with geographical objectives is to apply for approval and support from the RGS. If this is successfully granted, after interviews by a panel of experts and consideration by the expeditions committee, the job of raising funds, obtaining political permissions and persuading sponsors to donate goods and services to the expedition is greatly eased. We were an official RGS expedition and so had a head start, receiving in addition a grant of one thousand pounds from the Society's funds. Nevertheless, the organization, planning and equipping of such a large undertaking was still a major operation and this was done throughout by my indispensable right-hand man Nigel Winser. He had previously organized several undergraduate expeditions in Africa, usually from a call box in the passage of a student hostel, so he was confident that, with a prestigious address and a permanent office, he would be able to obtain most of our needs free.

There always seems to be a very good reason why the precise moment an expedition is planned is the worst possible one from the point of view of sponsorship. The economic situation in Britain in 1976 made ours no exception. Raising the finance for the expedition was, inevitably, the greatest single problem. Algy Cluff promised to underwrite a substantial part of the cost and it was his confidence in us that encouraged me to carry on when it looked as though we would never succeed.

Many firms were extremely generous in response to Nigel's powers of persuasion, giving us large quantities of strong plastic bags, packaging materials and medical supplies as well as rucksacks, baseball boots, kitchenware, matches, cameras, oil, batteries and three outboard motors. Many others were only able to offer discounts on their goods. My policy was always to buy in Sarawak rather than in Britain, if the goods could be obtained there, and only to ship out items which were donated or vital. This was partly to reduce the many difficulties of transportation and packaging, but mainly so that our presence should be seen to help the local economy, rather than be a burden on it.

Food was, of course, one of the three major items in our budget, the other two being transport and wages for local help. Here I was lucky, in that Marika was well-known in the cookery world as food editor of the *Sunday Telegraph* and the *Spectator*, as well as the author of over a dozen cookery books. Thanks to her letters we received lavish supplies of pasta (British), soups (mainly Oxtail), breadmix, sugar, jams, Provita (soya bean meat substitute), Guinness and barley sugar. Unfortunately we had no idea at that stage how large the expedition would eventually grow. We were working then on the assumption that some forty people would spend about four thousand man-days in the field. The final figure was one hundred and forty people working for a total of twelve thousand days, and as a result many of our supplies ran out about halfway through. On the whole, I preferred that we should live as far as possible on local food, both because it made a more interesting diet which would be familiar and acceptable to those working alongside us and because it was clearly desirable to include as much fresh produce as we could. This meant a basic diet of rice, since, although the pasta made an excellent change, the local people never really took to it. The cost of rice increased during our time in Sarawak by some twenty-five per cent and the cost of living there was not low even at the start. Petrol was about 90p per gallon and local labour rates about £18 per week, so that raising the cash for our day-to-day existence was always our biggest headache.

Early in 1977 I made a final brief visit to Sarawak in order to finalize details with the government. Robb Anderson came with me to Kuching, where we had meetings to discuss the scientific programme with those whose departments would be taking part. I also met the heads of Immigration and Customs who advised me on the regulations we should observe. We looked into the possibilities of raising funds in Malaysia and of being donated some food, equipment and building materials by Malaysian companies. On the back of an envelope Robb sketched a suggested layout for our Base Camp and this became the blueprint from which we worked when we later came to build it. I went on to Miri where Shell, who had already agreed to donate an initial £5000 to our funds, spelled out the substantial support they were prepared to give us on the ground. This included free telex facilities to London, using

Lord Shackleton's offices at Rio Tinto Zinc as the link at that end, since the RGS does not have a telex machine.

I flew to Marudi for the day where I met the Resident Fourth Division, the District Officer of the Baram and Temonggong Baya, the paramount chief of the region, who gave his permission for our Base Camp to be built on land just outside the park.

On my return to England there was only a bare four months to make all the final arrangements. Whether we would be able to raise enough money was still very much in doubt and there were many moments when we had cold feet about the viability of the whole project. At the same time a new philosophy began to emerge in regard to the nature of the expedition, which affected our outlook throughout and which may provide a model for future major expeditions. Nigel and I accepted from the outset that our job, based at the RGS and with its wealth of experience to back us up, was to support the scientists and to make their often limited time in the field as productive and painless as possible. All too often busy, highly qualified people on expeditions have to spend a large proportion of their days making travel arrangements, recruiting labour, shopping for supplies, cooking, washing and doing all the other things necessary to support life. Our aim was to eliminate these demands on the scientists as far as we could, so that they could divide their time between work and relaxation according to their needs. We therefore set out to recruit a small but competent administrative team, some of whom might also do scientific work but all of whom should contribute financially at the same rate as the scientists to expedition funds. I felt this was important if we were to avoid too much of a 'them and us' attitude developing between the administrators and the scientists; it is also my experience that people who are paying for the privilege of working hard do so with much more enthusiasm than those who are being paid or who are simply along for the ride. Having too many volunteers along to help, however willingly, has sometimes tended to make expeditions unsatisfactorily top-heavy on organization and weak on scientific content. In the end, of the 140 people who took part for stays of one month to fifteen months, eighty-five per cent were scientists and only fifteen per cent administrators.

By 13 June 1977 we were as ready as we were ever going to be. There were still grave worries about finance but flights had been booked and promises made so there was no turning back. Leaving Nigel to tie up last-minute arrangements at the RGS and hand over the home office to Shane Wesley-Smith, I went to Brize Norton to catch the first of the many RAF flights we were to use. We flew as 'concessional non-fare-paying passengers', which meant that we took precedence over the indulgence flights granted to the families of serving personnel, who paid a small charge. We had always to remember that the RAF was not a commercial airline. No flight, nor our place on it, was guaranteed; if someone with a higher priority suddenly needed to fly then we would drop out. If the mysterious workings of Whitehall decided that a flight should be cancelled, postponed or its timetable advanced so that we missed it, there was no come-back. We were asked to report at a certain time and place when the 'powers that be' would take us under their wings and we were not then expected to change our minds or enquire too closely or too often about our destinies. Security and safety arrangements were understandably strict so that one of my constant preoccupations was, by memoranda and word of mouth, to urge our members to abandon their individual personae for the duration of the journey and to do everything possible to make it easier for those coming after to fit smoothly into the system. I found it hard enough to follow my own directives since I have a regrettable compulsion when travelling to try and circumvent the rules and find ways of improving on the arrangements which have been made for my comfort. The well-tried tricks with heavy and hidden hand baggage, late and even multiple check-in to avoid excess weight, cultivating air hostesses for little favours like seats with extra leg room or a spare one in first class and trips up to the flight deck for a word with the captain and a good view are almost second nature to me. The RAF flight staff were politely and firmly wise to all of them.

   We sat facing backwards, which is safer if one should crash, and no alcohol was allowed on board which meant that we arrived at our destination feeling much better than usual. In Hong Kong I stayed with Brigadier John Chapple whose Gurkhas there and in Brunei were to give us constant help with transport on the ground and with our incoming and returning stores. It had been hoped that the British Army might have been able to take part in the expedition, seconding men to work with us in the field. To this end we had been officially classified as an Adventurous Training Exercise but the Malaysian Government, expressing due regret, decided at the last moment that they could not allow this. Later, however, they more than made up for this heavy blow to our plans through the helicopter and other support they provided.

   On arrival in Brunei I regarded the expedition as having begun. This was where the majority of our members would first set foot on Borneo soil; indeed some of the more enthusiastic ones started collecting almost before they left the airport. Brunei is a British Protectorate surrounded on all landward sides by Sarawak. The 9000-mile R A F flight terminated there and due to political differences with Malaysia there were no onward commercial flights to Miri. The only practical way to continue was overland and since the R A F flight usually arrived at Bandar Seri Begawan in mid-afternoon there was never time to do so the same day. The route followed a dusty or, after heavy rain, deep and muddy track across two ferries over wide rivers and the border closed at nightfall (6 pm). Normally the Gurkhas provided a bus to take arrivals to the officers' mess at Seria where there was often time for a quick swim off the beach before remembering to put on a tie for a last civilized meal at a polished mahogany table laden with the silver trophies of past campaigns.

I was fortunate in having many friends in Brunei who, for no reward, as there was little chance of their being able to visit Mulu, interested themselves in our welfare, smoothed our passage and were to entertain many of us in an atmosphere far removed from the rigours of expedition life. They also gave or lent us much useful equipment, such as tools for our workshop, fire extinguishers, hammocks and date-expired but still edible 'compo' rations.

Driving across the border fetching and delivering members was to be a regular chore for the administration team in the Land Rover but on this first journey I had not yet received the vehicle from Shell and was driven in luxury in a new Toyota land cruiser. The track was in bad condition and so we drove along the beach, the tide being out and the surface much smoother. It runs in a series of gentle curves for some 700 miles along much of the north coast of Borneo; the South China Sea, dotted at this point with offshore oil rigs, stretches away to Indo-China 550 miles to the north, while south-wards the forest crowds forbiddingly to the water's edge. Overhead a vast expanse of cloud-patterned sky begins to give a sense of the scale of this land, a vast evergreen island flat around the coasts, with a jumble of rugged mountains in the centre.

Between the Belait and the Baram rivers where the ferries cross, a series of tea-coloured streams reach the shore where they die on contact with the sand, leaving treacherous soft spots in which unwary vehicles can become entrenched and covered when the tide comes in. A hundred yards inland the ill-used track crosses the streams on rattly plank bridges from which a fleeting glimpse may be caught of dark mysterious tunnels between water and over-hanging trees, conjuring up pictures of wading waist-deep through leech- and crocodile-infested swamps and subduing for a moment the most eager of explorers. Long-tailed macaques search for crabs among the flotsam and scamper safely away from the waves to sit in rows on the oil pipeline which runs beside the track. Halfway, at Sungei Tujoh (Seventh river) is the lonely border post, where I warned the Brunei and Sarawak officials that I was only the first of a host of eccentrics who would be coming and going through their hands for the next fifteen months.

2

The Way to the Park

JOHN Maidment, the then Head of Trade Relations at Shell Sarawak, was the key man in our lives at Miri. Having been with the company in Borneo for nearly twenty-five years his knowledge of political, economic and social affairs was unrivalled and his unfailing good humour and bonhomie were capable of unravelling every conceivable bureaucratic bungle that came our way. Known to all as Big John his brief seemed to be as big as his own expansive personality: from arranging every detail of a sudden visitation from the chief minister or high commissioner and the resulting receptions and dinners, to sorting out the problems of the local work force and instructing expatriate employees of the company about the country and how to behave in it. It was very kind of Shell to let us monopolize so much of Maidment's time and his own generosity was boundless. The study in his comfortable house in the attractive residential complex at Piasau, between the town of Miri and the refinery and offices at Lutong, became Nigel's and my base on the coast, where we were able to garage the Land Rover, make endless telephone calls and keep some clean clothes for official visits. His office, with his attractive secretaries Noriah and Aisah, became our daily link with the outside world over the two-way radio. Through it we were able to send and receive telexes and telegrams as well as to load John with innumerable chores which sound so easy when described but take so long to fulfil.

He took me on a tour of calls on the officials with whom we would be dealing in Miri: first, the Resident Fourth Division, a kindly man who asked only that he be kept informed of what we were up to and chatted amiably about our work over coffee and sweetmeats; then Frankie Nyombie and John Guan, the heads of Customs and Immigration respectively, who were henceforth to become the two safe harbours in a troubled sea of bureaucracy upon whom we always called first whenever one of us had to go to Miri. Officialdom everywhere in the world can make or break an expedition according to the whim of its representatives and their interpretation of the rules. Although we had a directive from the government indicating that we should receive certain concessions on import duties and visa requirements the delays and mountains of forms implicit in these were potentially Kafkaesque in their ramifications. Queueing at crowded counters only to be told that the forms have been filled in wrongly and new ones will be required from a stationer on the other side of town will try the most patient traveller, while the midday heat makes it progressively harder not to make the unforgivable mistake in South-East Asia of losing one's temper. Thanks to the patience and sympathy of Frankie and John, miracles were worked in Miri every time we had to go there.

In addition to citizens of Great Britain and the Commonwealth only those from Holland, Switzerland, San Marino and Liechtenstein may enter Malaysia without a visa. Sometimes a member from elsewhere arrived without having previously obtained one. Moreover he had signed the form at the border as a tourist when we were all there specifically as professional visitors. He must fly to Singapore for a visa and return, but had neither the time nor the money to do so. John Guan would fix it somehow.

At the last moment, as delicate plant specimens were about to be airfreighted urgently to Kew before they died, we would find that they could not go on board the plane without yet another form which could only be obtained in Kuching. Frankie would fix it and allow us to do the paper work later.

The Forest Department were our hosts in Sarawak. Their headquarters were in Kuching where Joseph Yong was Director of Forests. I had had meetings with him in his office previously and during the next year those of us who managed to make the expensive journey by air down the whole length of Sarawak to the capital always called on him first, for with him lay the authority for all we were doing. We saw much more of Paul Chai, the forest botanist and liaison officer to the expedition. He had been to Mulu before, and was to come up-river with me and help set things in motion. In the local Miri office I met some of the staff who were to work most closely with us. Haji Suleiman, the quietly spoken head of Fourth Division, had succeeded beyond my highest hopes in persuading several timber companies operating on the Baram to donate materials for building our Base Camp. Joseph Au, his energetic deputy, was one of those rare officials who always seemed to have all the facts at his fingertips and a telephone that never stopped ringing. Alfonso, Denis, Ricky, Lewiin and many others worked there too, as did Manaf Sairi and Wit Treygo of the National Parks and Wildlife Section, a branch of the Forest Department. Malay, Chinese, Kelabit, Iban, Melanau and Canadian volunteers, they illustrated the multi-racial blend unique to Sarawak where, in the wake of a hundred years of rule by the three Rajahs Brooke and seventeen years of being a British colony, no one race is dominant politically, economically or socially and, fortunately for us, English was still one of the two official languages.

Timber is, after oil, the next largest of Sarawak's exports and the Forest Department is responsible for supervising the concessions and management of resources. Worldwide concern over the rapid disappearance of tropical rain forests provided the main purpose of our expedition. The rapid rise in timber prices reflects the speed with which accessible and valuable trees are being cut down, putting pressure on the industry and governments alike to increase production yet further. It has been calculated that at the present rate of extraction nearly all the lowland forests will have been felled within ten years and most of the rest within twenty-five. The Sarawak Forest Department's efforts to conserve stocks and encourage regeneration are hampered by shifting cultivators who move in rapidly and usually illegally after some felling has taken place, along the roads built by the companies' bulldozers.

A network of national parks is one way of attempting to ensure that at least something will be preserved when the felling is finally finished. Sarawak's national parks are among the best in the tropical world and the government has been highly praised for its foresight in creating them. A notice on the wall of the Miri Forest Office proudly quotes from a UN report: 'No other country in SE Asia has shown such foresight in the control of its forests.'

The Baram is the second largest river in Sarawak. It is the homeland of the Kenyah, Kayan and related peoples, part of the proto-Malay indigenous population who spread there from the Kajan river in Kalimantan. They are riverine, longhouse people who love their river and call it by many names, disparaging as well as proud and poetic ones. It is called Telang Usan which means 'the juice of the pineapple' but they also call it 'the silver snake' and 'the rainstream'. The original Baram river is a tiny stream at Marudi which used to be called Long Baram and then later, when it was the capital and administrative centre of the region, Claudetown. There is no road to Marudi yet which accounts for much of its charm, contentment and self-sufficiency. A daily flight in one of the Britten Norman Islander aircraft of the local service operated by MAS, the national airline of Malaysia, takes only ten minutes to cover the twenty-five direct miles from Miri airport; but first-time visitors should always take one of the express boats running upstream from Kuala Baram, the mouth of the river, which follow its great serpentine loops inland, making ninety miles of the journey and taking three hours. They should travel on the roof, rain permitting, in order to escape the drumming of the powerful diesel engines and the heat inside, but beware of the sun which burns even through heavy clouds. So many of our new arrivals suffered in this way on their journey to Base Camp that we came to identify the ailment as 'Baram nose'.

Atap palms (*Nipa*), the leaves of which are used for roofing, and edible sago palms (*Metroxylon*) line the bank in a solid wall at first, their stems growing straight out of the water. They dip and sway in the steep-sided wash as the express passes. Later, when the banks begin to show, they are eroded and the damage the wash causes can be seen. The government is trying to reduce this by limiting the size of the boats and telling the operators they must change to craft which are less destructive, but the rivers are still the main means of internal communication and it is hard to see what could be done unless entirely new forms of transport such as hovercraft are tried. Occasional longhouses break the splendid monotony of the scene, fronting straight on to the river, a fleet of longboats moored below them around which a splashing horde of naked brown children swim and play. Here the express will nose skilfully in, touching the bank long enough for passengers to step off over the pointed bow. Rafts of floating logs neatly tied together stretch for hundreds of yards behind a Chinese launch labouring under full power to tow them down to the sawmills. They seem motionless, but it is a skilful business and often there is a small boat with outboard motor worrying at the tail of the raft like a terrier to prevent it swinging out and colliding with the shore. 'Sinkers', giant logs from hardwood trees heavier than water, such as *keruing belian* and some species of *meranti*, are carried on great metal barges stacked high around a mobile crane which travels on board to load them on and off.

All sense of time, direction and distance is lost as the express forges its way through the hot, humid air of the coastal plains and swamps and arrival at Marudi is a welcome relief. Here for the first time a bluff rises up beside the river with three attractive old colonial buildings on it. Each one figured in our Mulu lives. First and grandest is Fort Hose, its cannon commanding the now much narrower river. Built by Charles Hose who was Resident of the Fourth Division from 1888 to 1904 it still houses the District Office, although the divisional headquarters was moved to Miri after the development of the oilfields. Hose, although he had failed to obtain his degree as an undergraduate at Cambridge, was later made an honorary Doctor of Science there (in 1900) for his pioneering ethnological work with the Kenyahs and Kayans. Although blaming the migrating Ibans for causing trouble among the resident populations it was in fact he who first introduced Ibans officially into the Baram.

Next to Fort Hose lies the Marudi Forest Office where Albert Klumai and his staff, whose resources we must have stretched unbearably with constant radioed requests for boats and drivers to supplement our own rather unreliable transport arrangements, always did their cheerful best to help, although their boats were somewhat heavy and their drivers nervous of rapids and of sleeping at our Base Camp, which they regarded as suspect and possibly dangerous territory.

Third comes the Rest House, previously the Residency, where traces of the terraced gardens can still be seen around the wide shingled eaves of the building and whose spacious verandah still affords one of the finest views of the Baram. Presided over by the delightful Mrs Lee, most of us spent our first and last nights in Sarawak under the slowly revolving fans in one of the four-bedded rooms with polished wooden floors and a glimpse at dawn of the Mulu range emerging above the morning mists shrouding the river.

Below the bluff lies the central market square surrounded on three sides by rows of what seemed at first identical Chinese shops, where we learnt that with practice and patience almost anything could be obtained; and on the fourth side by the busy and crowded waterfront. Here we were to do the bulk of our weekly shopping. I had planned at first, and budgeted accordingly, that we should only send a boat down to Marudi once a fortnight for supplies and to collect new arrivals. But as numbers increased and with them the demands on our commissariat, few weeks were to pass when there was not some urgent reason for a visit to Marudi. The discomforts of the long journey down one day and the slow, heavily loaded slog back up river again were offset by the opportunity of an ice-cold beer and a dish of succulent Baram prawns in one of the many small restaurants in the market.

Our local agent was an enterprising and energetic shopkeeper called Johnny Leong, who had had the initiative to write to me in England offering his services. He had suggested that he supply labour, river transport, building materials, camping and kitchen equipment, a house in Marudi, fuel and even aeroplane charter. Knowing him I am sure that, at a price, he could indeed have produced all he offered. However we could not afford the luxury of such grandiose sub-contracting but had to beg, borrow and, only when absolutely necessary, buy everything for ourselves. Johnny's shop nevertheless became our base and rendezvous in Marudi. New arrivals, dazed from their exposure on the express and still suffering from jet-lag, were directed there to find Johnny with a baby on his hip, a sheaf of unpaid bills in one hand and a telephone in the other, shouting in Chinese to a prospective customer, while a tribesman from far up-river wearing a hat decorated with beads, and quite possibly making *his* first visit to Marudi, stood patiently holding a packet of biscuits and waiting to be served.

'I didn't see Robin or Nigel yet, but maybe Sandy somewhere. Take my truck and leave your *barang* at the Rest House. No problem-lah.'

One of the nicest things about our time in Sarawak was that everyone used our first names throughout. Government ministers and radio operators, labourers and shopkeepers never tried to wrestle with our surnames and with one like mine this was a great relief. If flattery or special respect were being shown a 'Mister', 'Doctor' or 'Tuan' might be tacked on the front but the general informality helped to bridge cultural differences.

Many people warned that Johnny would take us for a ride and indeed, while always checking prices elsewhere, we did tend, for convenience and speed, to leave much of the shopping to him so that by the latter stages of the expedition our account with him grew alarmingly. But his generosity and helpfulness well offset any profits he made from us and the services he provided, such as free access to his truck, storeroom and telephone, were never charged for.

After my first night in the Marudi Rest House and a morning spent in meetings and shopping, Paul and I set off up river in one of the Forest Department longboats. For an hour or two the Baram continued to meander between wide sandbanks, and we passed the mouth of the Tinjar river on our right before turning left into the narrower and even more convoluted Tutoh. At Long Linei, a large timber camp, we stopped as I had arranged for thirty drums of fuel to be delivered there by Shell. We planned to fly them from there to Base Camp by RMAF helicopter as well as planks and roofing materials donated to the expedition and to the national park by some of the timber companies in the district. The RMAF had requested that we check that there was room for two helicopters to land so that the aircraft engines could be switched off if the need arose. Then if it should fail to start again a second chopper could fly in and start it with jump leads from its own batteries. There was indeed a broad open field by the camp buildings with a buffalo wallow in the middle, but I was dismayed to see that it was piled with stacks of colossal logs which looked as though they would take weeks to shift. Mr Wong the overseer calmed me down by fetching and demonstrating another colossus, one of the largest machines I have ever seen with a mighty mandible on the front which could lift the recently felled forest

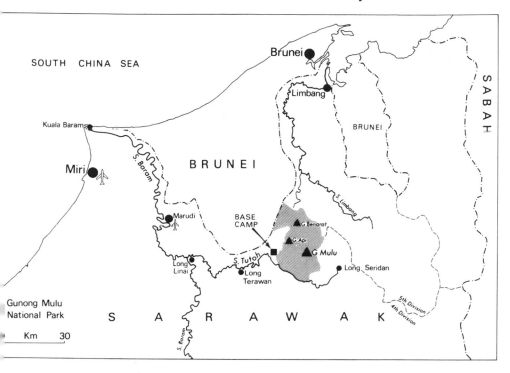

giants like matchsticks and either drop them in the river if they were 'floaters' or stack them elsewhere if 'sinkers'. 'Very quick. Soon move. No problem-lah.' This expression was to become our most used catch-phrase. Even when there *was* a crisis (and we faced at least one almost every day) 'No problem-lah' helped to defuse rising irritation and to put things in perspective.

Life in the timber camps was hard with few comforts or opportunities for relaxation. The management was usually Chinese and the labour often recruited from the Ibans. Melanaus and other coastal peoples although some local employment was also provided. Their job was to extract as much valuable timber from each concession as quickly and economically as possible and the destruction caused in the process by the bulldozers and the network of earth access roads was offensive to those of us concerned about the degradation of the environment and the loss of habitats for plants and animals. None of this, however, was the fault or concern of those actually doing the work and we always received generous hospitality and help from them. In return we were able sometimes to give them lifts on the river and occasionally sick people were brought to our doctors. Operating chainsaws, dragging logs through the forest and rolling them into the river were all dangerous jobs and we heard stories of horrible accidents, but they were a cheerful crowd who always waved as we passed by and were happy to help us out from the company store.

That night Paul and I stayed at Long Linei in one of the rough plank sheds, sharing the meal of rice and fish cooked by an elderly Chinese man. Few women ever join in the tough lonely existence of these camps, though our female members were, as everywhere in Sarawak, always treated with perfect courtesy. At dusk flying foxes (*Pteropus vampyrus*), the largest of all the bats, began to stream past overhead. With wingspans of up to four or five feet they were on their way from the trees where they roosted by day to their chosen feeding grounds, fruit trees planted near a longhouse on the river or a wild fig whose crop was ripe somewhere far in the interior. As they flapped past with slow steady wingbeats, looking like sinister props in a Dracula film, Mr Wong hurried for his shotgun and started trying to shoot them. They were flying at about maximum range so he was unsuccessful, although he did hit one which limped off into the distance like a Lancaster bomber with two engines put out of action by flak. Although flying foxes are said to make good eating and so, in Mr Wong's case where fresh meat is in short supply, it may be justifiable to shoot them, the sportsmen on the coast are hard to excuse as many of the bats must be wounded in this way.

In the morning we continued up the Tutoh to Long Terawan, the Berawan longhouse nearest the park, where we were to recruit most of our labour. The Berawan are a small group of about 1600 people. They probably reached the Baram shortly before the Kenyah and Kayan some two hundred years ago and they used to be classified as a sub-group of the Kenyah as they were thought to have many linguistic and cultural similarities. They, too, have a tradition of having come from the Usun Apau plateau but recent research by Peter Metcalf into their burial rituals and language has indicated that they are a distinct people. They now live in four main longhouses on the Tinjar and the Tutoh and they call themselves Melawan, but the Malay version of their name, Berawan, is more commonly used. John Proctor worked hard at compiling a substantial Berawan vocabulary of some 1800 words which is to be published by the Sarawak Museum Journal in due course. During several long talks with old men from the longhouse, and especially Tama Kasip the oldest inhabitant who, at the age of eighty, was still the Tua Kampong or headman, John was able to estimate that some of their ancestors first moved up the Tutoh to settle near the mouth of the Melinau in about 1863. After some thirty years they returned to a site further down the Tutoh where they remained until 1944 when their longhouse was burned by the Japanese occupying forces as a reprisal for guerilla activities. Shortly afterwards they moved to Long Terawan. The thirty-year-old longhouse there, when we arrived, was in the process of being abandoned and a new one built alongside a palatial modern building which Temonggong Baya, who himself came from Long Terawan, had had constructed a short distance downstream. This was causing some disturbance to their lives and most of the population were living on their small farms scattered along the river bank. The old longhouse, on an attractive site where it stretched far in each direction above the river with a row of tall coconut palms in front, was already looking sadly neglected. Over the next year we were to see it almost entirely dismantled and the materials taken to the new site. This lay some five hundred yards back from the river on a small hill from which a magnificent panorama of the Mulu range could be seen on the horizon. The Berawans understandably regard the lowland northern and western parts of the park as their territory and many know the region from having hunted there, so that they were the obvious first candidates to provide the bulk of our workforce.

The Temonggong was away in Kuching so we spent the morning discussing wage rates and travel arrangements with Philip Ube his agent and the longhouse entrepreneur who ran a Chinese launch which provided the only usual means of transport between this quite isolated population and Marudi. The Temonggong had also requested that Philip should be permitted to run a small shop for our employees at Base Camp which seemed a good idea as it would relieve us of the need to supply the men with food and other necessities.

At this time and indeed throughout the duration of the expedition I was regularly called on to make a formal speech explaining our purpose in being there, our hopes for the future of the national park and our desire that we would be able to work amicably and fruitfully with all concerned. My Malay was just adequate for this and most of the population of the Baram spoke it at least as well as I, but many, especially the younger generation, also spoke excellent English and it became easier to use one of them as an interpreter to translate direct into Berawan. The park had only very recently been gazetted and the Berawans were still unsure whether its existence represented a possible financial boom from rich tourists or something they should resent due to the potential farming land they had lost.

Back in the longboat I was at last about to cover the final stretch to the edge of the park and the future site of our Base Camp. After Long Terawan the Tutoh begins to narrow, twisting between low hills and foaming over shallows. There was not much depth to the river as there had been no heavy rains recently so that progress was slow and even dangerous with an outboard motor as, if the propeller should strike a rock or gravel, a shearbolt would break and all control be lost. This usually happened just as we were nearing the top of a rapid when the water was shallowest as it spilled over a shelf before rushing down into turbulent waves. Then, in order to prevent the heavy longboat being swept away downstream and perhaps capsizing if it lodged against a sunken tree, we would all jump overboard and either hold it against the current until the shearbolt had been replaced or, if it looked as though it would happen again at once, we would slowly heave it step by step towards the smooth water ahead. The force of the current against our legs and the uneven bottom made it extraordinarily difficult to keep our footing and produce a useful push so that we found as often as not that we were holding on in order to remain upright. Only the skill and strength of the Berawans who had come with us from the longhouse ensured that we always got through in the end. Islands and gravel banks divided the bed of the river into a number of channels which, even when we came to know them well, could change overnight after a flash flood so that it was necessary to learn to 'read' the water as well as to remember the best route. We came to know each of the fourteen rapids intimately, giving them names and numbers according to their characteristics. They stretched over twenty-five miles guarding a progressively more interesting and less disturbed landscape. Parts of the bank were now covered in primary forest with tall trees festooned with hanging creepers and luxuriant parasites, sometimes a blaze of orange flowers.

As the mountains, whose shapes were to become so familiar to us, drew nearer the rapids worsened until, the last Berawan farm far behind us, we turned into the cool tunnel of the Melinau river. The contrast with the wide, turbulent, muddy Tutoh was dramatic. The water was dark and limpid, so clear that fish could be seen darting away as our boat passed over them. The trees met overhead in places and the forest seemed at last primeval and undisturbed, full of cries of birds and the hum of insects, yet at the same time still and mysterious after the constant chatter of the Tutoh shallows. Round the first corner a limestone cliff rose sheer like a castle covered in vegetation. Soon after another crag, deeply undercut by the current, towered on our left. A short way on, perhaps a mile in all, and a third and even more imposing cliff, this one hung with stalactites, marked the spot where we were to live for more than a year.

3

Base Camp

OPPOSITE the cliff was a yellow sandy beach, the first true sand I had seen since leaving the coast some 180 river miles away. A neat flight of steps with handrails painted green led up to a small incongruous bungalow which had been built two years before to mark the establishment of the park but had only been occupied for the odd night by survey parties and government botanists. Beside it a tangle of felled trees and the sound of a chainsaw marked the site being cleared as a helipad. We clambered over the heaped branches to shake hands with the eight figures, stripped to the waist and streaked with sweat and sawdust, who greeted us. David Labang and Manaf Sairi with six Berawans had arrived the day before and had already made great progress. Everyone stopped for a welcome break and tea was brewed while we had our first conference together. There was so much to plan and it seemed impossible that we could achieve all that had to be done before the first scientists arrived in a bare three weeks' time but we were all filled with enthusiasm and confidence. Four more helipads had to be cleared at strategic points around the park where materials for sub-camps could be flown and from which the scientists would work. The site for the Base Camp had to be cleared and the longhouse we were to live in erected. Stores and supplies had to be brought up-river, labour recruited, trails to be made and marked, radio communications set up and dates for airlifts fixed. Members of five different races, we represented the various elements which would have to fuse together if the expedition was to be successful.

Paul Chai, Chinese, an outstanding botanist with an important government job, had the dual responsibility of liaising with us on all matters both bureaucratic and scientific. Slim, round-faced and youthful, he carried an authority which we were to exploit unmercifully, leaving him to represent our interests in Kuching, explain away our mistakes and pass on our many requests for official help.

David Labang, a Kelabit from the remote Bario highlands of the interior, a people who have leapt with unique energy and success into the twentieth century since the Second World War, was undoubtedly the finest field zoologist in Sarawak and worked for the National Parks and Wildlife Section in Kuching. He had studied at Kuala Lumpur University with Lord Medway* and taken part in a great many field trips both in Malaysia and Sarawak. Gentle of manner but utterly fearless in the jungle or when handling snakes and other venomous wildlife he, too, was to fulfil two roles. A key member of the zoological programme he also spoke Berawan and Penan and was admired and respected by both for his highborn position in a neighbouring society and for his knowledge and sympathetic understanding of their lives. He was our ultimate intermediary in local affairs and also contributed valuably to an appreciation of the knotty problem of man's impact on the park, both past and future.

Manaf Sairi was a Malay from the coast, also with much field experience. He too worked for the National Parks and Wildlife Section but in their Miri office and was therefore to have an intimate and continuing association with Mulu which was administered from there. His job was to help us prepare the ground for the national park's future so that the facilities we established for our own work could be taken over and used to best advantage after we had left, when in due course the park would become accessible to the general public. Life in the interior is never easy for a Muslim, as pork, the main source of fresh meat, and utensils which have previously come in contact with it, are unclean for them and may not be consumed or used. Manaf's good humour and tolerance helped us all to understand and respect these matters and to avoid embarrassment when others of the same faith joined us.

Inggan Nilong and Usang Apoi were half-brothers from Long Terawan. Inggan, whose grandfather had guided Lord Shackleton on the first ascent of Mulu, was later to be elected by the men as their leader and official spokesman. He was the strongest man I have ever known, a gentle earnest Hercules of five foot six inches, unfailing and untiring in his loyalty and concern for our welfare. Usang was in many ways his opposite: a brilliant craftsman bursting with character and resourcefulness; but somewhat devious and always with an eye to the main chance.

I was British and the appointed leader of our enterprise. Very conscious of their superior expertise and experience in almost every field, I could only admire the workings of a multi-racial society, and meanwhile hope that they would continue to give their advice and help so freely. The beginnings were certainly auspicious. Accommodation was cramped but everyone seemed to know exactly what to do and all were experienced at living rough.

* Now the Earl of Cranbrook.

We dined on rice and salt fish and we talked far into the night by the light of a kerosene lamp.

We planned to build our house on the far bank at the base of the limestone hill. The land was a little higher there and so less liable to flooding during the heavy rains to come. Taking a ball of pink plastic string and the sketch Robb Anderson had drafted earlier in the year I crossed over to begin marking out the ground plan. A huge fallen tree trunk led at a gentle slope into the water and made an excellent landing stage to which boats could be tied and up which stores could be carried much more easily than by scrambling up the muddy bank. Above the bank a dense wall of foliage obscured what lay behind as it does almost everywhere on the rivers where man has not cleared it. Having cut a path through, however, I found the undergrowth sparse and could see some way between the boles of the tall trees and saplings. Pacing in twenty-five yards, which seemed a comfortable distance to be away from the river, I tied the string to a tree and attempted to measure fifty yards parallel to it. I soon ran into trouble, meeting an impenetrable tangle around a recently fallen tree where spiny rattans and tough broad-leaved plants were already striving to reach the small patch of daylight exposed above. Two of the men came over from the helipad to help and with *parangs* we cut a way through. I now worried about aligning the house so that the minimum number of large trees would have to be cut down. Not only would this make our work easier but, if left, they would provide shelter and shade for us. Although the ground plan covered 1000 square yards I was able to work it out so that only seven major trees needed to be felled, but lining up the angles without theodolite or set square kept me running around all day paying out pink string and getting in a frightful tangle and sweat. While casting about I came on the remains of a Penan camp. The poles were rotted and collapsed, proving that it had been abandoned some months earlier but it was the first indication that there were Penan in the area and I wondered how long it would be before they showed themselves.

The site seemed a good one with fairly level ground and the prospect of a view of the mountains when the river bank was cleared. A channel with stagnant water in pools ran round the back, coming from behind the limestone hill, so that during floods we would be on an island. There was a danger of mosquitoes breeding in these pools and drainage was going to need careful planning, but on the whole I was well pleased.

Leeches seemed especially prevalent on the Base Camp site, though after it was cleared they vanished. That first day my legs and arms became covered in them. Later Manaf's wife was to supply us with home-made 'leech guards' which gave almost complete protection. They were simply two pieces of cotton stitched together in the rough shape of a Christmas stocking, worn between sock and boot and tied below the knee outside long trousers. Setting off in a clean white pair we tended to look like Morris dancers and felt a bit foolish at first but almost everyone came to swear by them. Not that the bite itself did much harm and removing them was always easy by pulling them off between finger and thumb or scraping them with a knife (it seems to be a fallacy that they will leave their heads behind) but the continued loss of blood from the bite of a well-established leech, that has had time to inject its anti-coagulant, was messy and there was always a danger of the wound developing a secondary infection. Leeches lurk under leaves or on the forest floor waiting for a warm-blooded creature to pass, for they appear to feed only on blood. When they sense the approach of a potential prey, either through vibrations or heat, they stand up rigidly on the hind sucker, leaning in its direction. As it passes or stops near them they will then wave and lash excitedly from side to side, reaching out as far as possible if on a leaf, or looping across the ground in a sort of demented one-legged goose step. Only the barest contact is needed for them to latch on to their victim and hoist themselves upwards until bare flesh is found or a convenient crevice in clothes where they can hide until an opportunity presents itself. With most leeches there is no pain as they sink their sharp little fangs in and begin to feed, so that they may continue to do so for a couple of hours, swelling in the process from a slim worm-like creature to a bloated black slug two or three inches long. One species, however, which had attractive longitudinal yellow and green stripes and which we called the tiger leech, gave a sharp nip at the moment of truth and thus was usually discovered immediately.

Leeches have been very little studied since they are not known to transmit any disease and so have never drawn much attention to themselves except as a minor irritant. Sue Proctor later made a collection of the different species brought into camp by members and kept them alive in humid conditions, starving some to see how long they could survive without blood and feeding others. Sundays were leech-feeding days when she would solicit volunteers and only those who had had the foresight to find urgent business elsewhere or were prepared to suffer the scorn of their associates were spared. The leeches were placed on arms and legs and encouraged to set to work. Depending on how hungry they were and the palatability of their host this might take some time; when they started feeding, a number and the time was written next to them on the limb with a felt pen. They took so little blood that the sacrifice was only a small one, although the wound would bleed rather disgustingly for some time afterwards. Some status could be gained by selecting the larger and stronger specimens but only Sue's husband John and I achieved the ultimate accolade of becoming 'three tiger-leech men'.

That first evening I climbed the little hill beside our camp, for the first time, scrambling over the sharp limestone and reaching a spot where on one side a cliff (*batu* in Malay) dropped sheer a hundred feet to the river below and on the other a magnificent panorama of the Mulu range was laid out. The gorge carved by the Paku, a tributary of the Melinau, formed the centre of this spectacular view framed by two-thousand-foot white cliffs. To the right the main ridge of Mulu itself could be traced to the summit cone while on the left the notched and craggy silhouette of the unclimbed Gunung Api suggested how arduous travel there would be. Between our *batu* and the hills and stretching away to the horizon on either side lay lowland forest broken only by occasional steep limestone outcrops. From this vantage point we could look down on to the upper canopy of an endless variety of trees, their colours changing with the seasons as some flowered, fruited or shed their leaves; birds and monkeys could be observed through field glasses roosting or feeding and the evening exodus of around a million bats from the Deer Cave provided a climax to one of the finest views obtainable anywhere for those lucky enough to observe it. The only sad note was struck by the knowledge that most of the lowland forest did not lie within the boundaries of the park and was likely to be felled in time. Much of it was already part of a timber concession and the effects of logging operations were bound to be significant not just on the scenery but also on the wildlife and perhaps also the micro-climate and vegetation of the park itself. We later built a small camp on this site and made an easy path to it so that members could escape there in a few minutes to sit and watch or work. At dawn and dusk especially the changing light and cloud effects, captured so successfully by the BBC team in their film of the expedition, were breathtaking. Most of our time in the rain forest was spent below the canopy of the trees, a fascinating, teeming environment but a dark and sometimes forbidding place with a horizon limited to a few feet, where we grubbed about for weeks on end collecting, recording and making observations. The view from the *batu* never failed to uplift our spirits by giving a wide perspective of the dramatic and dynamic terrain in which we were privileged to study.

Before the Base Camp could be built the site had to be cleared and the planks and zinc sheets for the floor and roof brought up-river.

Helicopter support had been requested because it would be virtually impossible to transport the permanent building materials to the sub-camps by any other means. Carrying load after load of heavy planks and zinc sheets far up Gunung Mulu and across the rivers between the furthest point boats could reach and the Melinau Gorge would need an army of supermen. This was a task the RMAF had agreed to undertake as their contribution towards the establishment of the national park. We had asked if it could be extended to include carrying in our first batch of fuel and some of the materials for Base Camp. Before the airlift could begin, however, the helipads at the sub-camps had to be cleared and levelled. Originally there were to be four of these up the mountain (Camps One to Four) and a fifth in the Melinau Gorge (Camp Five), but when it came to the point we found that there was no suitable flat ground at Camp Two or Three and to clear sufficient land on the ridge at either camp would necessitate cutting down too many large trees. We calculated that it would take at least two weeks to clear each site with a team of six men. Our agreement was that, since we would be using the sub-camps for the next fifteen months before handing them over to the National Parks Department, we should pay for the labour whilst the Forest Department would supply the materials and government officers to supervise the work. Manaf was to take on Camp One, Ricky Nelson and Lewiin Roman from the Miri office Camps Four and Five respectively, while David Labang built an emergency pad near the top of the mountain. I discussed the design of our Base Camp longhouse with Usang and allocated him a team to start preparing the ground and to cut poles from the surrounding forest with which to build the framework. The sub-camps were intended to be permanent so the timber for them had to be treated but, since the Base Camp was to be removed when we left, the quality of the materials used was less important.

I now had to return to the coast to meet Nigel and Clive who were due to arrive with our first batch of stores from the UK. Also due was the jet boat which Hamilton Marine of New Zealand were lending us for the duration of the expedition. This worked on the principle of sucking water in through a grille underneath, driving it through a turbine and forcing it out through the stern, thus eliminating the need for a propeller and so making the boat able to travel fast in very shallow conditions. A revolutionary form of transport designed for shooting the many formidable rapids on New Zealand's rivers, we hoped it would relieve us of the necessity of hiring longboats and labour to drag them over the hazardous shallows below Base Camp. John Hamilton himself, the head of the firm and winner of innumerable international speedboat races, came with his son Michael to break it in and show us how to drive and maintain it. I met them in Miri; we lowered the gleaming white boat off the deck of the freighter, on which it had been shipped, straight into the water of the Miri river. They started it up and began to demonstrate its remarkable capabilities to the press and invited guests from Shell and the government, flying over the shallow sandbar at the river's mouth and turning it at speed in its own length.

Leaving them to make some modifications in the Shell workshops I took the Land Rover to Brunei. Clive went on ahead by express and longboat to convert part of the national park bungalow into a laboratory while Nigel and I cleared the first two hundred boxes of stores through customs and began the long hard process of transporting them up to Mulu. They came across the border on a fleet of lorries to Kuala Baram where we loaded them on to a large Chinese launch, one of the flat-bottomed, diesel-engined craft with a high wheelhouse which ply the Baram and which was going up to Marudi that night. We followed next morning in the jet boat, going out to sea before turning into the Baram and reaching Marudi in only three hours from Miri. There we had to unload everything – it came to about six tons in all – on to the dock, sort out some of the less essential items and carry them across Marudi to Johnny's store, meanwhile negotiating with another small Chinese launch called the *Bee Lian* which, we learnt, was due to go part way up the Tutoh and which would save us an expensive charter. Pausing for a moment to wash off the sweat we sat on the bank watching the throng of longboats below and a sizeable steamer moored at the main customs dock. Marudi is a registered port served by some shallow-draught sea-going vessels which always looked out of place so far inland. We were able to send some freight by sea but ships only go to the Far East intermittently now from Europe and usually by indirect routes so that the RAF was much quicker and, of course, free.

A Chinese launch pulled out into the stream and began to forge against the current, the noise of its engines echoing off the far bank. 'Isn't that the *Bee Lian*?' asked Nigel. It was and we raced for the jet boat, overtaking her before the first bend in the river and forcing her to return and take on our boxes. She was off to supply one of the timber camps on the Apo, a tributary of the Tutoh and her captain was reluctant to take on more cargo. But we talked him into it and arranged to off-load everything again at the mouth of the Apo. After she left the jet boat began to give trouble so that we struggled painfully after her, stopping time and again in the broiling sun while John and Michael tried everything to locate the fault; replacing parts of the engine, blowing through fuel lines and testing the ignition. Several days later they traced the fault to a minute filter in the carburettor which was being clogged by dirty petrol. But that night we limped up to the Apo long after dark to find that we had overtaken the *Bee Lian* without knowing it in a heavy rainstorm; we spent an uncomfortable night in a deserted hut, wet, cold and hungry. Shortly after we had settled down on the dry earth floor some Kayans from the nearby longhouse at Long Panai arrived, having heard the sound of our engine, and tried to persuade us to return home with them.

By then we were too tired to move again but sat talking with them far into the night discussing the possibility of their transporting our boxes the rest of the way to Base Camp in a fleet of longboats.

Long Panai was a fine new longhouse of some thirty 'doors' – that is thirty families each with their own accommodation and all under the same roof – leading out on to a communal gallery with kitchens and washrooms behind. It was agreed with the headman when I called there next day that three longboats and nine men would be available but not until the following day, Monday, as they would not work on the Sabbath, being good Christians. We therefore loaded everything off the *Bee Lian* on to the bank, left Nigel to guard it, and the Hamiltons and I reached Base Camp in a slightly healthier jet boat. Among our first batch of stores were two inflatable rubber dinghies and two $9\frac{1}{2}$ hp outboards donated by Yamaha.

When I returned next morning we found that the three longboats and the jet boat could not manage all that we had to transport. Nigel and I decided therefore to inflate one of the rubber boats and run in one of the engines by driving it up the river. It was one of those days when everything goes wrong. We found that a vital part of the engine had been sent ahead with the longboats; it was excessively hot, there was no shade and assembling the boat took longer than we expected. The engine did not match the boat as well as we had hoped and it would barely plane over the water; we were both overtired from the heat and lack of sleep and in danger of becoming irritable. But it was also Nigel's twenty-fifth birthday and I had promised him that somehow we would reach Base Camp that day. By dusk we were barely into the series of rapids and through ignorance of the channels and the exceptionally low water we began to break shearpins on the bottom. When this happened we found that a rubber inflatable is even harder to hold against the current than a longboat. The only thing to do was to let it be swept back down into calm water again and our progress was very slow. Quite suddenly it became so dark that we could not see one end of the boat from another, so further advance was impossible. With false optimism and without a torch, I said we would just wait until the moon rose before going on, so we curled up in the bilges, soaked to the skin and rather cold and slept for three hours.

We woke at 11 pm to find bright moonlight shining through a haze of mist over the river and glinting off the waves. We groped our way over only two more rapids before finding the entrance to the Melinau. Everything was silver and black, the leaves etched in a glittering tracery against the sky, the trees dark silhouettes and the water still as ebony in front and broken milky waves behind. Miraculously we hit nothing as we sped over the surface to reach the camp five minutes before midnight.

Over the next three weeks we built the longhouse. Usang was a master builder, accepting our eccentric design without question and working tirelessly. He selected suitable timbers for uprights, framework and eaves, set some men to cutting them into correct lengths and others digging holes into which the main supports were to be sunk. He measured everything by eye, arm span and rule of thumb, standing on a trestle with the heavy chainsaw, wielding it almost like a paintbrush to cut and notch the poles so that everything fitted together. The sounds of hammering and sawing drowned the background din of the forest and in what seemed like no time our extraordinary dwelling began to take shape.

There were ten rooms, each large enough to sleep four, with partitions between them six feet high made of *kajang*, panels of tightly woven palm leaf. In front of them a wide gallery ran the whole length of the house with an open dining area in the centre leading between a roomy verandah in the front and the kitchen and stores at the rear. A solid raft supported on empty oil drums was connected to the bank by a cleverly designed flight of steps which slid across it when the river rose and joined a raised walkway to the house. At the back another walkway led to *jambans* or latrines built over deep holes dug in the soft earth, and the generator house. Further pits were dug for rubbish which was burnt in them with the help of kerosene every other day.

The roof was made of lightweight zinc sheets and sloped one way only from twenty feet above the ground at the front to twelve feet behind the kitchen. We would have preferred to use *atap* – the local palm leaf thatch – all over both for aesthetic reasons and because it would be cooler in the heat of the day, but we were advised that this would be sure to leak and in any case the zinc was donated whereas we would have had to buy *atap*. When the really heavy rains came we were glad of the choice. Only the verandah roof sloped towards the river and this we did roof in *atap* so that, with a further 'fringe' along the front of the main roof to deflect the rain outwards and give some shade, none of the zinc was visible from the river.

The floor was raised six feet above the ground leaving ample storage space underneath and guaranteeing that we would be above the highest flood. Rainwater was collected off the roof into tanks by the kitchen and piped to a shower room beside the store and there was also a wash house on the raft. A hollow iron pipe found in the Tutoh, relic of a long-forgotten oil-prospecting party, made a fine bell to summon us to meals when we sat at a long narrow table voraciously consuming vast quantities of rice, supplemented with fresh fish or wild boar if our hunters had been successful, fried Spam or other tinned meat as well as fresh vegetables and fruit from Marudi or from our own garden. Jo Anderson, biologist from Exeter University and one of the early arrivals, designed and built a clay bread oven out of an empty oil drum and mud so that fresh bread could be baked regularly as well as pizzas and macaroni cheese.

Marika, who came out with our children for a time early on, had been given a wide selection of seeds by Suttons and took a special interest in creating a vegetable patch and seeing what would grow. Courgettes, aubergines, tomatoes, peppers and beans were especially successful but radishes, although they shot up, were soggy and small. Root vegetables were a complete failure. Unless carefully tended, plants ran riot, strangled by weeds and devoured by insects. As a result our garden grew in fits and starts as keen horticulturalists came and went. The Berawans regarded the fruits of our labours as common property, helping themselves as crops ripened, and we never managed to beat them to the bananas and sweetcorn they had planted along the bank. When the little papaya tree Marika brought from my cousin's garden began to bear fruit, I jealously numbered them with a felt pen.

We went on improving, altering and adding to Base Camp right to the end but, as soon as the main structure was built, we sent out invitations for a longhouse-warming party. Scientists had begun to arrive and a party was a good excuse for us all to get to know as many of the people in Sarawak connected with the expedition as could manage to join us. On these occasions it is customary to roast a buffalo. I tracked a suitable beast down at Long Terawan but the going price of about £200 was not included in our budget. Hans Brinkhorst, the Managing Director of Shell Sarawak, generously agreed to buy it for us, bringing a dozen of his senior staff in by helicopter for a day and a night.

Abang Muas, the Deputy Director of Forests, also flew in by helicopter with Abang Kassim, the National Parks and Wildlife Officer, Paul Chai who had by then returned to Kuching and Haji Suleiman from the Miri Forest Office. Temonggong Baya headed a group of about sixty Berawans and brought a quantity of *borak*, the strong home-brewed rice liquor with which he toasted us one by one, while Apa, a stout smiling Kayan, sang our praises. The Temonggong made a speech of welcome and formally named the house Long Pala, meaning 'the place of the head', as many heads were buried there after being taken in battle. He told us that his grandfather once killed a dozen government officials from Brunei there but one escaped and reported the incident to Rajah Brooke who jailed his grandfather for a year in Kuching. It seems this story may be apocryphal, however, and confused with another incident when the Berawans were themselves attacked by Ibans. 'In any case,' he said, 'we don't take heads any more. Rather we look forward to working with you.' A new longhouse should really have a human head buried under the main upright but as a symbol I hung the gory head of the buffalo over the entrance where it stank and dripped until we could bear it no longer and sank it in the river tied to a rope. Some weeks later the skull, picked clean by the fishes, was retrieved and restored to its place of honour.

We feasted and danced, made more speeches, drank the rest of the *borak* and a fair proportion of the lager and stout donated to us by Guinness and tried to explain to everyone what we would be doing in Mulu for the next year. Suddenly it began to seem too short a time for all we planned.

4

Personalities

I HAD very little to do with the selection of participants. This is unusual; the traditional image of an expedition in its planning stages being of the leader interviewing prospective candidates at the Royal Geographical Society and, by a few shrewd questions, assessing how well they will stand up to the rigours of the particular environment into which they are about to plunge. By careful character selection and the blending of harmonious types he attempts to build up a cohesive team which will pull together through thick and thin. Even in novels this process is seldom made to work and in real life the records are full of personality clashes ranging from major rows, such as the Burton-Speke affair, to the members simply not wishing to meet or speak to each other again once it's over. As with arranged marriages so with expeditions; the members themselves are often the last people who should be consulted as to the composition of the team and the leader need have little more than a power of veto and the right to include those for whom he sees a particular need.

As a member of the expeditions committee I was involved in the planning from the beginning but the choice of members was always a matter of who was the right person to fill a scientific role and whether they were available; and this worked. There really were no serious rows and I believe that a quite unprecedented number of lifelong friendships were forged.

When a new group arrived Nigel or I would usually meet them at Bandar Seri Begawan airport in order to see them through the rather tortuous route to Base Camp. Most we had never met before. Like the first day on board ship at the beginning of a cruise we would look each other over and wonder how we were possibly going to put up with such clearly incompatible companions for the next few months. When the time came round for us to see them out of Sarawak again and put them on an outgoing flight there was hardly an occasion when we did not say 'I wish you weren't going so soon. It seems to have gone like a flash. Do come back if you can' – and we meant it. This was largely due to the professional approach of all participants. They had been chosen because they were good at their job or expert in their discipline and their prime objective was to get on with it. Everyone had had to work hard and often make personal sacrifices in order to raise the funds needed for their financial contribution to the expedition's budget and as a result they wanted to make the most of their time. Few were motivated, as is often the case on other expeditions, simply by a desire to have an exciting time in an exotic environment; indeed their very professionalism and expertise made them better able to appreciate the fascination and interest of this beautiful country than the average tourist or explorer. Too many people on holiday or adventure safaris become wrapped up in the mundane business of simply travelling and fail to observe what they are travelling through.

Having been granted an unique opportunity to live and work in one of the richest and most fascinating environments on earth we were determined that every scientist taking part should be given the maximum help to achieve as much as possible in the time available. Members arrived to find labourers, often chosen with their special needs in mind, ready to work with them. Rations could be put together quickly if they wanted to go straight off into the field where reasonably well-equipped sub-camps awaited them. A doctor, and often a nurse as well, ran a well-stocked clinic at Base Camp and it was reassuring to know that in case of accident or serious illness medical evacuation by helicopters, thanks to the flying doctor service and the RMAF, could be arranged at short notice.

Machinery, such as outboards, generators and chainsaws, was maintained and serviced throughout the year by Philip Leworthy who paid his contribution to the fund for the dubious privilege of doing a job unrestricted by fixed working hours and often unprotected from the elements. He was always ready to have a stab at repairing cameras, tape recorders, torches, Tilley lamps, flash guns, altimeters and any other bits of scientific equipment which broke down under the strain of heavy use and an unfavourably moist climate. Usually to be seen seated on the verandah floor with his long legs extended across the passage so that anyone passing had to jump over and so scatter the bewildering array of bits and pieces spread around him, he had the true engineer's patience and tolerance of the average man's ignorance and the obduracy of inanimate objects. He also had a remarkably high success rate.

We tried to make life at Base Camp as pleasant, comfortable and relaxed as possible so as to provide a contrast with the relatively hard and often lonely life at sub-camps. Key elements in this were the skills and personalities of our successive cooks. They too, to my retrospective amazement, contributed financially and they were all winners, getting up before anyone else so as to have breakfast ready by 6.30 am and barely letting up throughout the day and evening until those working late had had a last mug of Milo. Their sole rewards were an occasional dash up the mountain or a re-supply run to a sub-camp and a very occasional shopping trip to Marudi, but they were all unfailingly cheerful and even grateful for the opportunity of taking part.

The first, and the one who probably had the hardest job, was Rosemary. She arrived before the longhouse was completed, before gas cookers replaced our first slow and smelly kerosene stoves and she had to design and supervise the building of the kitchen. Used to helping on her family's sheep station in New Zealand she was well able to cope with the early primitive conditions. She set a standard which was never lowered.

Marika helped her for a time, adding ambitious touches of *haute cuisine* such as liver paté from wild boar, saddle of python stewed in a pressure cooker and marinated river carp. She was also there to unpack many of the supplies generously donated by British food firms in response to her deter-mined efforts on our behalf. Had the expedition remained its originally-planned size these would have been almost enough to feed us for the whole fifteen months, supplemented only by fresh vegetables, fruit and a few essen-tials from Marudi. Our food costs rocketed from March 1978 onwards when members increased dramatically and our original donated stores ran out.

Australian Kate, who came next, supplemented her skills in the kitchen with a remarkable talent for caricatures in pen and ink; in addition, to the great delight of many of us, she played classical fugues on her recorder down by the river. Her stay included Christmas, when all the eagerly awaited special luxuries such as plum puddings and crystallized fruits failed to arrive due to a hold-up in the RAF – they were eventually eaten with undiminished relish in March – which meant that she had to improvise with a local turkey from Marudi, wild pig's ham and, so I am told, *borak* butter on the home-made pudding.

Next came Uschi, a curvaceous Swiss strudl whose speciality, apart from apple pie (using pineapples) and *rösti* (using yams instead of potatoes), lay in cuddling the depressed and making the lonely feel loved. I should add here that the communal nature of life in our longhouse made it impossible for relationships between the sexes to develop beyond the merely flirtatious. Married couples were much teased during relatively dry periods when the deafening sound of torrential rain on the tin roof was not heard for nights on end. Wives and sweethearts left at home may be reassured by this if they are worried by photographs they may have seen of our penultimate cook, the long blonde Rosie from Tasmania, which show her sunbathing on the raft in her apology of a bikini. She stayed with us the longest of all our cooks and I heard no complaints about that.

Finally there was Wilma, married to our last doctor and a doctor herself, but as willing and imaginative a cook as any. She proved that even the cook's life could be hazardous when early one morning she was bitten on the finger by a nine-inch centipede lurking in a tea towel. This is said to be about the most painful thing that can happen in the Borneo jungle. She tried her best not to scream and wake everyone as her hand and arm rapidly swelled and the agony shot through her body. Her husband Alan gave her an injection to send her to sleep and no permanent damage was done.

A succession of charming and conscientious Berawan and Penan girls came to work at Base Camp during the year. Esther, Imelda and Judy from Long Terawan could each have run the kitchen on their own and indeed soon learned to provide meals of an equal standard to our imported cooks when they were temporarily away. Sarah, Arun and Ting came from Long Iman and during my early talks with Tuwau, the headman there and Sarah's father, we agreed that they could learn a lot that would be useful to them after we had left by helping our cooks and doctors. I think on balance the encounter was of value to them but the outward manifestations were not immediately an improvement. When I first visited Long Iman they had glossy long hair hanging over bare shoulders to a colourful sarong. By the time we left they had all had their hair cut and permed, wore flashy modern clothes – usually T-shirts over tight trousers – and were seldom far from their transistor radios playing loud Western pop music. The most appreciated work they did was undoubtedly the same-day laundry service which they somehow managed on days when the sun shone. There is nothing worse on an expedition than having to spend much of one's limited spare time washing filthy muddy clothes. Instead, after being scrubbed in the river, they would appear on the laundry shelf neatly stacked and even looking pressed through being properly folded. There was a certain wastage from garments floating away downstream or not being marked. St Michael underpants were particularly susceptible to incorrect identification, and every now and then we would hold a jumble sale to clear out unclaimed clothes from long-departed members, but by and large this was one of the best features of Base Camp.

The people who are responsible for the paperwork form the core of any expedition. Shane Wesley-Smith and Sandy Evans alternated throughout; one holding the fort at the RGS where a high level of diplomacy was needed not to disturb the calm of its august portals as lorry loads of food, equipment and often badly packed personal possessions had to be sorted and stored before being transported to Brize Norton, while the telephone lines hummed with distraught wives and parents who hadn't heard from their loved ones, or with members checking their travel arrangements. Meanwhile the other was always in the field supervising the labour, helping with the mass of correspondence which arrived every week from all over the world and checking that everything needed was available. Their characters differed radically but they provided the buffer between us and the world outside and helped to give the expedition a human face to our friends and sponsors.

Shane, ebullient and cheerful, with a talent for charming helicopter pilots and government officials, approached the whole business with the determination of a vicar's wife organizing a local fête. Her tendency not to tolerate fools kindly but to treat us all like delinquent schoolboys kept us on our toes, though one or two of our senior scientists did look a little harassed when told off for not ordering their packed lunches far enough in advance.

Sandy, who gave a first impression of being unable to organize a gumboot-throwing contest, always seemed to get it done in the end. It was a relief to have someone to blame when things went wrong even if, as was usually the case, it was not his fault; and he was immensely popular on the Baram. Without speaking a great deal of Malay he seemed to know and be known to everybody. On his birthday he received an alarming number of affectionate cards from young ladies in several different longhouses as well as from those who attended both Marudi's high schools.

The lynch-pin upon which the expedition depended, and to whom almost the entire credit for the success of the organizational side must go, was Nigel. He always seemed to know exactly what was going on and was never anything but calm and cheerful no matter how great the crisis or the provocation. He worked tirelessly, at first in London setting it all up and obtaining a rich Aladdin's cave of useful stores and equipment, from paper clips to outboard motors, from manufacturers who do not give easily today unless convinced that they are dealing with an honourable man who will repay their generosity with publicity and field reports. In Base Camp he almost never seemed to sleep. Night after night long after everyone else had gone to sleep a light would still be burning in his *bilek* as he wrote letters and reports, prepared labour charts and wage sheets, wrestled with accounts and tried to foresee and forestall every conceivable problem.

Our first doctor, Gerry Mitton from South Africa, made an inauspicious start, arriving in a dazzling yellow trouser suit with ten suitcases of elegant outfits given her for publicity by a fashion house. On the way up, after fetching her from Marudi in the jet boat, I had to call in at Long Terawan and, saying I would only be a few minutes, I left her sitting in the sun. Thinking to go ashore she started to walk across the slippery notched pole leading to the bank only to fall off into four feet of soft black mud. Watched by an interested group of children she stripped off, washed everything and was sitting demurely in the boat almost dry again by the time I returned. Base Camp was far from ready then and she was not impressed. 'Utter chaos' it may have been, but she did not endear herself to me by saying so, pointing out the deficiencies in our hygiene and the health risks we were running. Then she set to work and seldom paused for the next three months. Her room at the end of the longhouse was also the clinic and as word of her skills spread increasing numbers of patients came to see her. Malingerers and those with minor ailments were firmly told to go to the excellent government dispensary down on the Apo which she visited, establishing lasting friendly relations with Henry Peng, the dresser there. The ladies of Long Terawan prevailed on her to visit them regularly. She became a great favourite with all along the river and was the first of us to be honoured by 'naming ceremonies' given by both the Kayans and the Berawans who called her 'Bungan' meaning 'flower' in Malay, after a legendary heroine of theirs. During some of the most critical times of the expedition she was a tower of strength, working day and night when a measles epidemic hit the Penan who had little resistance to a disease new to them. Some would have died without her treatment but none did. Meanwhile she cooked when we were cookless for a time, operated the radio and ran the camp if Nigel and I were both away. First appearances can be deceptive.

Her successors maintained the standard that she set while David Giles, a GP from Bude who was also with us for three months, excelled, being very strong and fit and so able to cover large distances at record speeds, in ministering to the sick in the field. Our most dramatic rescue occurred when a message arrived by runner to say that Ben Lyon, one of the toughest and most experienced of our cavers, was sick with a fever in one of the most remote and inaccessible parts of the park, Hidden Valley, a deep cleft in the limestone behind Gunung Api, which we had only reached for the first time a few weeks before. David set out on foot carrying the thirty-five-pound medical pack and guided by a Penan. Eleven hours of hard walking later, he takes up the story:

On arrival I found what should have been a robust, cheerful speleologist/climber, director of a Cumbrian outdoor pursuits centre. In a few days he had become a feeble, dehydrated, grossly depressed mental and physical wreck, incapable of any but the smallest movement. General physical examination and four-hourly recordings suggested Dengue fever, but there was no question that such an unbelievably weak man would be able to leave this hazardous physical environment on his own feet for at least two or possibly three weeks. The camp site was at the base of the valley with cliffs of two and a half and three thousand feet along two sides – the most spectacular limestone scenery – and the site was surrounded by very dense primary jungle. Trees were up to 150 feet high and the base of this forest was covered in thick rotan and vine up to about six or seven feet high. In short the jungle was about as thick as it becomes in this part of the world. The man had to be moved and we had to attempt it by helicopter. However there was no helipad.

He sent a runner back with a note requesting Medivac in twenty-four hours. Since I knew there was no helipad there and it seemed likely the patient would have to be winched out I contacted the RMAF. Meanwhile David and the three remaining cavers with their three labourers began to try and clear a landing site:

Matters were further complicated by the fact that we had no felling axes or chainsaws, only five *parangs* to do the cutting work. It seemed a Herculean task but the Europeans had decided to do it and with encouragement from the two Berawans and the Penan it began to seem that it might just be possible. The fit speleologists were tough lads and used to very hard physical work in the Derbyshire coal mines. Together we were able in fourteen hours of continuous cutting, sweating, blistering and swearing, being scratched, torn and bitten by various insects, to clear a pad of some twenty-five yards in diameter with something like an approach path for a helicopter. The last 120-foot tree was felled twenty minutes before the arrival of the rescue plane. Following a short flight I was able to settle in the sick man at Long Pala where a little comfort was available both for him and his medical adviser. I am glad to report that within three weeks he was back in his caves.

I flew in with the rescue team to guide the pilot to the spot since I was the only person to have been there before. We found the tiny clearing they had made with such effort and it looked quite impossible for a helicopter to drop down the narrow funnel through the trees. I fully expected the pilot, Lieutenant Tengku Adnam, to turn back but with consummate skill – at times the rotor was no more than six feet from the trees – he pulled it off. He was later awarded a medal for this feat.

John and Sue Proctor with their daughter Katy were among the first scientists to arrive and they stayed until the end. John, an industrious Lancastrian and a lecturer at the University of Stirling, never stopped work for thirteen months. Even during all-night parties at Long Terawan he grilled the Bera-

wans on their history, practised their language in which he became suffi-
ciently fluent to make speeches and further earned their high regard by his
remarkable capacity for *borak*. It is a matter of honour with the Berawans
that their guests should pass out as a consequence of their hospitality but
John, perhaps due to an early training on North Country ales, was seen on
more than one occasion to be still on his feet at 6 am. During meals his distinctive north country accent could usually be heard through the chatter discussing abstruse matters of science or planning the next day's work.

Sue, who helped John in the Forest Ecology Group project by spending
untold hours in the laboratory sorting and weighing litter samples as well
as doing her own zoological work, was a passionate ornithologist. The sighting of any strange bird would bring her running, binoculars at the ready,
especially when the bat hawks swooped and stooped among the evening flight
of spiralling bats. Their daughter Katy, who had her second birthday three
months after arriving, proved a huge success. She seemed to thrive on the
environment, confounding those who had doubted the wisdom of having one
so young on an expedition. An enchanting child, she contributed greatly to
the morale of her many and varied temporary aunts and uncles and played
happily for hours with the Berawan and Penan children. Insects and other
creepy-crawlies held no horrors for her. She positively *liked* leeches, which
she collected and looked after with a devotion most children reserve for
kittens and hamsters. On Sundays she was the first to tender a chubby arm
at feeding time.

John and I were in a minority among the long-term Base Camp residents
in preferring to remain clean-shaven. Harry Vallack, John's assistant, like
Nigel, grew such dense black whiskers that he almost seemed to disappear
behind them, a disguise which accorded well with his reserved and amiable
disposition. When it came to organizing our own entertainment or singing
in the evening, however, he was a natural Master of Ceremonies and as Father
Christmas for the children of Long Terawan he was a triumph. Mark Collins,
whose long-term project on soil fauna, particularly termites, complemented
John's work, favoured a Van Dyck beard which gave him a *farouche* air as
he diligently examined the endless specimens collected for him by his team
of helpers. His energy for travel both in and out of the park, combined with
his skill as a climber and enthusiasm for his subject, meant that he covered
an amazing amount of ground at great speed and with no fuss, as well
as being an excellent ambassador for the expedition when he extended
his research to timber camps and lectured on our behalf in the coastal
towns.

Our other enduring member was Kevin McCormick, a Canadian ornithologist, who lived a solitary life except for a Berawan helper, for nearly a year at Camp One, only returning to Base Camp every two weeks to re-equip and spend a couple of nights in relative luxury. In spite of his lonely bachelor existence he was always immaculately turned out and seemed oblivious to discomfort.

I could devote the rest of this book to descriptions of our Berawan and Penan friends and helpers. So many of them became our close companions working alongside us, making camp in the forest, our welfare and comfort their constant concern. Few scientists ever asked us to allocate different men to them when they returned from a stay at sub-camps and many developed lasting friendships. I hope that they too may remember us with the same affection now we have all left, for without their help and guidance we would have achieved little. The older Berawan and the Penan seldom spoke any English, but their skills as trackers and guides were greater and so they tended to work with members who already spoke Malay, had been in Sarawak before or were seeking to collect or study animals or plants which required special knowledge for identification. Berawan men, once married and with children, are properly addressed by the designation 'Tama' followed by the name of their first-born. Thus Inggan Nilong should be called Tama Bulan or 'Father of Moon' since his eldest child was a daughter charmingly so called. She in turn was called Bulan Inggan and her children would in turn adopt their father's first name as their second one. For convenience we tended to stick to original names on lists and wage sheets since these were usually the ones they themselves gave when signing on; but we tried to learn their new names as well and address them by these in conversation for politeness. It was not as difficult as it sounds to remember two names for people.

Lang (Tama Iring) was our most experienced hunter and woodsman. Very quiet and dignified he said little but was greatly respected by the other Berawans who elected him their second spokesman. He nearly always worked with zoologists, helping to mist-net birds, trap animals or identify footprints. Leloh, a recently-settled Penan from Long Iman, was an outstanding expert on plants. John Dransfield, the palm expert from Kew, was surprised to discover as they worked together that Leloh had names for almost all the wide variety of rattans in and around the park, even ones for which he had no use. Some were, he said, especially good for particular purposes, such as making the frame of a *selabit* or woven back-pack, while others were used for the fine decorative work or for baskets, weaving, selling down the river for eventual use in furniture making; and some even had excellent fruit for eating. This sort of information is, of course, extremely interesting and useful to a botanist and can often be acquired in no other way except from a local expert. Those with skills as fishermen helped collect specimens as well as supplement our diet; Penan were asked to reverse the dart in their blowpipes so as to stun lizards without hurting them; all were constantly questioned about every conceivable aspect of our environment with which they were far more familiar than we could ever be.

The younger Berawans had markedly different characters from their elders. Many had only recently left school, spoke good English, were less surprised by our peculiar areas of research and in some cases became very interested themselves in what we were doing. They were a cheerful, noisy crowd, always keen to have a party, pore over pictures and diagrams of animals and insects, climb mountains or explore caves while carrying heavy loads uncomplainingly for hours on end. At the same time they retained the courtesy, good manners and honesty inherent in longhouse life. We all lived very much on top of each other, whether in Base Camp or in sub-camps, with our possessions spread around and shared; items that must have been very tempting to people rapidly acquiring a taste for modern goods such as watches, cameras, radios, imported clothes, books, fishing tackle and tools were left lying around. Yet nothing was used without permission being asked and, although inevitably things did disappear occasionally, nothing was ever stolen.

The mutual trust which developed between us all; the knowledge that we did not have to worry constantly about checking our possessions, hiding or locking them away; the easy familiarity between people of so many different races and backgrounds; these are the things that we will all look back on with most pleasure when we remember our time in Mulu.

5

The Park

THE overriding, ever-present, feature of life in a rain forest is the sound it produces. Before dawn, wherever I slept in Mulu, consciousness would come suddenly: no gradual surfacing through layers of sleep or sloughing off of scattered dreams which even on a clear spring morning in the English countryside is normally part of my waking; but an instant awareness of familiar yet often unidentified noises. The distant roar of traffic in a city, for all its horn blasts and sudden screeches, lulls because it is inanimate; the background roar of the forest, while often strangely similar, is alive and the louder cries and songs which rise above it spell fear or death, lust or the joy of life.

Slipping quietly to the ground so as to leave others sleeping a little longer in the longhouse, I would reach for my towel and pad down the walkway to the steps above the river. Mist rising from the water gave a slight chill as the sky lightened, throwing the trees across the river into relief. The first bird called, clear and lucid, the familiar four notes from Beethoven's Fifth Symphony dropping surely out of space to greet the day. A babbler of the genus *Malacoptera* – we called it the 'Beethoven bird' – sang each morning loud near the camp or far away and almost inaudible, sometimes a bit off key, sometimes with a note of madness creeping in, as though being condemned to a constant opening bar for eternity was taxing its sanity.

Rapid movement behind the mist as the sandpipers went past, flying a zig-zag course in tight formation to their feeding grounds somewhere upriver. At first, in July and August, they only came in twos and threes but later, when the migrants arrived, the flights increased to eight or ten. In the evenings the same groups would dart past again heading downstream to their roosts on the Tutoh sandbanks. As the sandpipers vanished, a brief white ribbon undulated along the dark trees opposite, as leisurely as a lady floating a silk handkerchief from a carriage window or dangling a pale hand in the water beside the Shalimar; a male paradise flycatcher, its long white tail streaming, flew to its nest to relieve its dowdy mate.

I would wash, dipping a bucket in the river and hesitating for a delicious moment before emptying it over my head. Fish hurried to the soap. The Berawans were moving by now, smoke curling through the thatch. One or two would join me on the raft to wash or bale a longboat of the night's rain and paddle silently off to inspect their nets. The summit of Mulu was just visible from the camp and the sun rose behind it. To improve the view we built a platform thirty feet up between three small trees next to the longhouse and called it Camp Seven. From there, as the layers of mist before the mountain rose like theatrical backcloths, changing colour from blue to mauve to pink, a series of delicate Chinese watercolours was created, cool and elegant as silk for a few moments before the inevitable harshness of the day. With the sun a yellow bulbul (*Pycnonotus zeylanicus*) would begin its extravagant song from a dense thicket beside the water. Smythies in his *Birds of Borneo* accurately described this as 'a prolonged series of magnificently warbled notes, richer and more powerful by far than the songs of such celebrated performers as the nightingale and blackbird but lacks variety and is always sung fortissimo'.

The cooks now rang the gong and everyone in camp came running or shuffling according to their temperaments. Plans were made the night before but they always needed changing in the light of day. Sabang was needed as a boatman so Mark, who was off to Camp Five for ten days, would have to take Silat instead which meant an advance of cash for Silat so that he could buy food for the stay. The other men were sharing out their loads on the verandah, packing food and clothes into the excellent Manor plastic bags which proved one of our best sponsored goods. White, tubular and very durable they slid neatly, singly or in pairs, into rucksacks or could be tied to rattan *selabits*; they kept all water out even when dunked in the river. Longboats were loaded to take those going off on the Mulu trail to Camp One or beyond up the mountains across the river or, if the water was high, some way up the Paku to save trudging along the muddiest and worst bit of the path. Then the boats came back to collect the Camp Five party who had anything from one and a half to five hours sitting on the hard, narrow stretchers (depending on the state of the water) before reaching Long Berar and walking for another two or three hours to the camp.

Meanwhile, Nigel or I would try to get through to John Maidment on the radio. This involved concentration, good timing and a certain amount of aggression, as there might be up to twenty other operators waiting to jump in the moment the current conversation finished. Since that conversation was probably in Chinese – Foochow usually – it was hard to judge when it was nearing its end but on the magic words 'over and out' a score of voices started to shout 'Miri Control' – though some had trouble with their rs and ls – followed by their call sign. Ours was nine one six; sometimes we would repeat it for an hour or more before receiving an acknowledgement and sometimes none would come at all if a valve had blown and we were not transmitting. On raising John there might be a telex message to receive or send, each letter laboriously spelt out in a hotch-potch of Alpha Bravos, problems to resolve or news of new arrivals or helicopter flights. We sent few non-vital messages to our families at home, not because John objected to doing so but because spelt out like that they seemed frivolous halfway through, especially as we knew a horde of eager fingers attached to listening ears were poised over transmission buttons waiting for us to finish.

Base Camp would empty through the week to fill again at the weekend. There was always too much to do; work in the laboratory, repairs to machinery, walkways, roofs, buildings; new buildings for increased numbers, boat journeys to fetch and carry or to fish; photography, writing, medical crises, letters, reports and back to the radio. Everyone seemed to want to visit as much of the park as possible during their stay so that whenever things began to quieten down a new party would prepare to set off. On the rare occasions when it looked as though we actually might have a really quiet day to catch up with things, a crisis *always* occurred.

A small Penan boy, Tawee's son from Long Iman, was brought in by long-boat and carried up to the verandah. He had been bitten on the toe by a black snake, probably a cobra, and already after only half an hour his foot was swollen to twice its normal size. The wound itself had been smeared with powdered 78 rpm gramophone record, a well-known local cure for snake bite, probably because it has a caustic effect and burns off the surrounding skin and flesh. For once there was no doctor or nurse in camp but a notice had been pinned on the wall with instructions for what to do in such cases and we followed them.

SNAKE BITE

1. Sit down and remain as quiet as possible for 20–30 minutes.

2. Take some form of anti-histamine and anti-pain preparation if they are available.

3. Tie a tourniquet above the bite if possible. This should only be tight enough to make the veins swell a little and should be removed for a few minutes every 15 minutes.

4. Above all DON'T PANIC! Remember death from snake bite is very rare – so take it easy.

1 Motor-powered longboat on the way to Base Camp

2 The foothills of Gunung Mulu seen from the Batu at Base Camp

3 Building Base Camp

4 Base Camp in the rain. In times of heavy flooding the river rose as much as eighteen feet, to within inches of the raised floor

5 Base Camp cut off from the outside world except by river or from the air

6 A ten-door longhouse on the banks of the river became home for the expedition's scientists

7 Rugged landscape in the park

8 Local Berawan craftsmen building one of the expedition longboats from a single tree trunk

9 Longboats were used not only for re-supply but also to take scientists further into the forest

10 The author (*left*) and Nigel Winser with the supplies needed for one person for fourteen days in the field

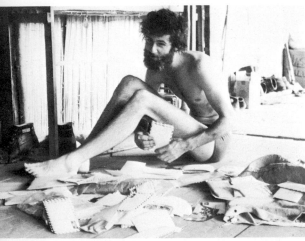

11 Philip Leworthy sorting the post

12 Marika Hanbury Tenison baking bread in an oven made from an old oil-drum and mud

13 ABOVE LEFT Lord and Lady Hunt (*left*) with Air Commodore Sam Welsh of the Royal Malaysian Air Force at Base Camp

14 ABOVE RIGHT The author and his deputy Nigel Winser with members of the Sarawak Soil Survey Team

15 The Mulu Expedition, May 1978

16 Gunung Mulu with Hidden
    Valley in the foreground

17 Nigel Winser among the
    limestone pinnacles

We sat with him loosening the tourniquet every fifteen minutes and keeping a chart of his temperature until at last he dropped off to sleep.

Next day Rosie the cook, who was also a trained nurse and had returned from climbing the mountain, took over. At first all seemed well then the swelling began to move up the leg and she said he should go to hospital. The jet boat was leaving early the following morning but it already had a full load of departing members who must catch their flight home from Brunei. There was room for one small boy but not for his parents who had themselves never been to Marudi and were appalled at the prospect of letting their small son go there alone. I had to spend much of the night reassuring them that he would be better off in a hospital than with us and that he would return. The danger was that he might collapse from shock and kidney failure which we had no facilities to deal with. At last they agreed that he might go but they wept and talked for the rest of the night and were inconsolable when he left. Happily he recovered in the Marudi hospital and returned a week later very pleased with himself and more grown up; but it had all occupied a lot of time.

In sub-camps we usually slept in what were locally known as hammocks–canvas stretchers along which poles were inserted and tied apart at the ends to make light, easily erected and fairly comfortable beds. I had some proper Brazilian hammocks which some of us used at Base Camp but which were not suitable for carrying into the field. The coldest camp was Camp Four at 5600 feet (1800 metres), lying at the end of the final ridge below the summit. Here sleeping bags were essential and we issued them from our store to any locals we sent there. It was a refreshing, even bracing place to work with superb views from the helipad across to Gunung Api and beyond to the coastal plains. At night the lights of the off-shore oil installations could even be seen sometimes but it was seldom clear for long: clouds formed rapidly sweeping up the steep sides of the mountain to obscure the top for much of the time. Below the clouds the moss forest grew: a weird fantastic place with gnarled roots and branches festooned with mosses and liverworts. On the main route ûp Mulu a path was cut, so that it was seldom necessary to duck or step aside. Trying to travel on other, unvisited, ridges through moss forest was like a bad dream. The tangle of soaking vegetation seemed designed to prevent one passing. Often the track of a small animal, probably a civet, would run along the ridge for a time and following this was like swimming underwater through thick seaweed. One became completely wet and coated in black mud, scratched by thorns and often suffered deeper cuts by using a sharp *parang* to clear a path in a confined space. Compensations were the absence of leeches at this altitude and the many brightly coloured plants growing there which were much more visible than lower down due to the small trees. Rhododendrons produced startlingly large, brilliant blooms of red, white, yellow or orange; orchids were a delicate white or green. One in particular reminded me of a hanging lily-of-the-valley: nepenthes, the strange pitcher plants, grew in such profusion that in places high up where the vegetation was very low and stunted they had crept over it in a solid flowering colourful mat looking like herbaceous borders.

It was good to arrive back in Camp Four after a day spent in such an environment, to be greeted by a roaring fire, and instantly proffered a large tin mug of tea (for which our men quickly learnt most of us had an insatiable craving at all times), dry clothes and a warm sleeping bag. Stretching out aching limbs on a hammock, examining and treating wounds, blisters and rashes was a wonderful relief; writing up notes by Tilley lamp or candle-light, eating rice and a dubious hot stew tasting predominantly of oxtail from a tin plate while the rain teemed down outside and thundered on the roof, these are things we will remember with varying degrees of affection and nostalgia. 'More rice, Tuan?' always asked anxiously, for we ate too little rice by Berawan standards and they always cooked too much by ours. Their capacity for rice amazed us while we often missed having more varied protein in our diet. I remember arriving at Camp Four, having spent a few days cutting a new route up the north-west ridge of Mulu, to find John and Barbara Croxall delightedly feasting on a giant rat which they had killed the previous night. The joints were small, but fresh meat was always a treat.

The morning calls of gibbons carried well to Camp Four from the valleys below, bird life was plentiful and varied there, the coolness made a pleasant change and it could be a good place to work undisturbed. But it could also be alarming. Landslides were very common high on Mulu, especially after heavy rain, reminding us that any steep slope with all its vegetation and anything standing on it, might take off at any moment with no warning. Ilkka Hanski tells of an afternoon at Camp Four when it began to rain so hard that the noise was almost unbearable and it was like sheltering under a waterfall. When it stopped, as suddenly as it had begun, he ran to the helipad to check the rain gauge there and found that an astonishing 4.9 inches had fallen in three hours.

Camp Five, down in the Melinau Gorge, had its attractions too. Here was the best swimming in the park, a clear, deep pool on a sandy beach into which the river splashed over warm rocks. Harry Vallack spent more time there than anyone else, checking the limestone and *kerangas* plots (see pp.

99–100) and welcoming those who passed through. It is an old camp site where the overhang at the base of the limestone cliff gives some shelter; it must have been used for centuries by the Penan. Being the only easy access to the wide basin behind Api and Benarat everyone and everything that wishes to go there must normally pass through the gorge. One morning while break-fasting in the large permanent camp we built there I saw a troop of about twelve maroon leaf monkeys (*Presbytes rubicunda*) come crashing through the trees in great leaps to stop at our clearing and examine us for some time without apparent fear before making a detour round us. Opposite the camp, high on the cliff face of Benarat, is a cave the locals call the Tiger Cave. They say that a tiger used to come out on the ledge at the cave mouth and could be seen lying there in the evening sun. It is not absolutely certain that there are no tigers in Borneo, though it seems most unlikely as there is no reliable evidence of their having ever existed in the past. But the indigenous people believe in them, have special names for them, can distinguish them quite clearly from the only known large cat in Borneo, the clouded leopard, and many places are named after tigers in both Berawan and Penan. This Tiger Cave, however, was inaccessible both from above and below, though presumably the tiger knew a way in, and so we were never able to examine its supposed lair.

The main disadvantage of Camp Five was that it was the worst place in the park for so-called sandflies. In fact these were small midges which bit persistently and almost invisibly in the evenings and from which many people suffered a lot of irritation. Another problem was that the Melinau river, run-ning through the gorge, could rise very rapidly, even when little or no rain had fallen near the camp. This meant that having waded across quite easily in the morning, holding on to the rope we had tied across for security, there was always a danger of being cut off by a raging flood in the evening. I think the luckiest outcome of the expedition must be that no one was drowned, as fording rivers in flood and capsizing heavily loaded longboats were constant dangers and the temptation was very great to take risks in order to reach the comfort of a camp rather than wait for the water to subside.

Probably the most spectacular spot in the park was about 3000 feet above the gorge on Gunung Api where a small temporary camp overlooked the famous Pinnacles which we adopted as the Mulu symbol. Geomorphologists became very excited by these dramatic needles up to 150 feet high, sculpted and grooved for fifteen million years since the whole limestone massif rose from the ocean where it formed from the remnants of sea creatures. No one knows exactly how they came about but they are unique in size and shape with edges as sharp as knives. The whole of the surface of the limestone mountains of Api and Benarat and the lesser outcrops around them are pitted and cracked with sheer cliffs, deep holes, strangely weathered rocks sometimes balanced on edge and ready to fall, with a tangled mass of vegetation growing wherever it is possible to do so and sometimes seeming to hold the whole together. But the Pinnacles are outstanding, even in this Disneyland environment, and no one who struggled up to the camp overlooking them could fail to be impressed by their sheer size and grandeur, especially when the setting sun made them cast their shadows far across the tops of the trees growing from the soil caught in the deep crevices near their base. They are among the wonders of the world.

The other world-class wonder, easily reached in the park, is the Deer Cave. Our speleologists, who should know, as they had already visited most of the other great caves of the world, maintained that it was probably the largest cave passage anywhere. An hour's walk from Base Camp it was only one of over a dozen major caves they surveyed during the three months they were with us in what they were excited to discover was one of the world's most extensive cave regions.

As the year went by we explored most of the park, making long journeys with suitable guides to open trails to new and often completely unknown parts, where even the Penan had not been before. Early on I felt it was important to tell as many as possible of those living in and around the park what we were up to. When David Labang returned in the autumn with his brother Lian we made a patrol of the northern part of the park where Robb Anderson and Paul Chai were at that time working in separate temporary camps on the vegetation survey. This was across the watershed and in the catchment area of the Limbang river so that it seemed a good moment to visit the Iban and Murut peoples there. Before setting out we had transmitted a radio message asking if a boat could be sent up the Medalam from the Limbang to fetch us but it seemed unlikely that it would be received. Therefore, when we reached the proposed rendezvous at the junction of the Medalam and the Terikan rivers after three days to find no boat waiting, David and Usang began to build a raft. They said that twenty lengths of bamboo were needed to support one man in the water. Since four of us were planning to go on the raft we cut eighty poles from a convenient bamboo grove on the bank. First four pontoons were made of bundles of twelve poles lashed together. Then a platform using another thirty was laid across the top, supported on two strong cross-pieces. Above this a smaller platform was built so as to carry the *barang* out of the water since with us on board the raft floated partly submerged.

The Medalam, down which we now floated and poled our way, has a quite different character from the Melinau. Instead of curling along under a limestone wall, trees meeting overhead to form a tunnel and with sandy bars and muddy inlets, the Medalam is a big, clear, boisterous river full of rocks and gravel beds. Fine trees line the banks, many with a red peeling bark like eucalyptus, and the open reaches are wide and deep. Rafting is the best way to travel a river, even though the Medalam had a few daunting rapids where we were nearly swamped; silently we drifted for two hours beyond the last boundary of the park at Long Mentawai seeing things a motor would have disturbed; a five-foot monitor lizard draped asleep in the sun over a submerged log; a green heron standing motionless gazing into the water; striped squirrels playing on a branch.

Then we heard the sound of a motor and ran into a party of heavily armed Iban hunters making their way upstream. David warned them not to go into the park, of which they claimed to have no knowledge, and not to use *tuba*, a poisonous liana which kills fish. It was very noticeable that there were already fewer fish in the Medalam, almost certainly due to the extensive use of *tuba* and we agreed that it was urgent that a post be established soon on that side of the park, as well as at the Melinau entrance, to protect it from illegal incursions. This was borne out during the night we slept and talked at Long Medalam, the longhouse on the Limbang where the Penghulu or senior chief of the Murut people lived. He too claimed not to have been told of the park, although it had all been legally cleared with him two years before. Ibans are moving into the Medalam in large numbers and we found some five hundred living there already. Clearly they pose a grave threat to the park if the law is not explained, wardens appointed and a ban on hunting, fishing and logging strictly enforced.

The Medalam was the route by which Spencer St John made the first attempt to climb the Mulu massif in 1857, although the mountain he actually reached was Benarat, still unclimbed today. In *Life in the Forests of the Far East* he describes a 'rocky eminence' through which the Terikan river passes first 'purling along to this lofty wood-crowned mass of limestone and then entering a spacious hall it was lost. . . .' He calls this place Batu Rikan but it is better known locally as Lobang China from the legend that once two intrepid Chinese merchants made their way there bringing a boat across the watershed, but not knowing the geography were swept to their deaths. We stopped there to look into the 'spacious hall' and it is impressive to see a river disappear, though the cave is hardly worthy of the name compared with those waiting to be explored in the main mountain. The place, illustrated by St John, where the Terikan (which he calls the Terunan) 'issues from the face of the precipice' was also as he says 'a fine sight, this body of water running impetuously from its natural tunnel: on either side lofty trees arose, and above the green verdure spread in masses'.

A week later David, Lian and I set out again to make the first complete circuit of the park. To do this we had to walk for six days eastward to Long Seridan across difficult country not previously known to any except nomadic Penan. We needed Penan as guides, but this was by now no problem as, after remaining hidden for the first two months of our arrival in Mulu, they had now begun to appear in numbers seeking medical help from our doctor and work. The first to visit our Base Camp was Nyapun, a strong and highly intelligent man who was to become my closest personal friend and confidant in Mulu. I asked him where he lived and he pointed north-east. Had he a family? Yes, two wives and ten children he told me with neither pride nor shame, speaking enough simple Malay for communication to be easy. Could I visit them? Certainly, he said, and we walked fast in single file for five hours with only one short ten-minute break. The Penan move through the forest in a different way from even the most skilled hunters among the Berawan or other longhouse people. The Penan seem to hear and feel everything that is going on around them and to be influenced by each sound and movement. Even when carrying a heavy load they do not keep to a steady slogging pace but pause to listen, turn aside to look, hesitate and generally make life difficult for one walking behind who may be trying to ignore his uncomfortable surroundings and simply get the journey over. It can be annoying at first and it takes time to learn not to be always in a hurry.

Nyapun's family had not, except for his eldest son, seen a European before, but they greeted me calmly, accepted my presents of sugar, salt and tobacco and fed me on heart of palm, sweetened brown sago, smoked mouse deer and river prawns. Their camp of three *sulaps*, low palm-roofed shelters on a raised platform, overlooked a shallow stretch of the upper reaches of the Lutut river where we bathed and the children tried to catch fish with their hands. The wives played on a bamboo instrument called *pagang* and danced in the firelight. Being truly nomadic their camps are built to last only three or four weeks before they move on to a new site. In the morning, with their few possessions – a couple of *parangs*, cooking pots and blowpipes with spear-heads attached being their only metal objects – they all accompanied me back to Base Camp. From then on others arrived until we had met over three hundred Penan who hunted and gathered wild sago in and around the park. Their future and the impact they are having, and will continue to have, on the park was one of the subjects which stimulated most discussion among members. The Sarawak Museum made a detailed study of the Penan as a part of the expedition and some of their conclusions appear in chapter 12.

One of the most intriguing places in the park was the blind valley we could see on the map and from the air behind Gunung Api. A whole segment of the Mulu watershed, a wide valley of streams and waterfalls, joined to form a river which entered a deep and narrow gorge in the eastern side of Api, the sides of which rose sheer for between two and three thousand feet. Unlike the Melinau Gorge, however, which cut right through the limestone range, this one stopped about halfway through the mountain and the river seemed to disappear underground. Robb Anderson, on an earlier visit to the park, had looked down into this remote and inaccessible spot and confirmed that the river did sink into a sump. Mark Collins and I were able to see round the shoulder of Api into the valley while trying to climb that mountain from the east, an attempt in which we failed by about four hundred feet to reach the top due to coming up against an unstable overhang.

We called it Hidden Valley. It was not until eight months after the expedition began, in February 1978, that, realizing the cavers would find much of interest there, I set out with three Berawans and a Penan to cut the first path in. We approached it from the south, turning off the main Mulu trail at Camp One and following the course of the Paku. The chief obstacle was a very steep-sided three-thousand-foot sandstone ridge running down from near the summit of Mulu to end abruptly against the vertical white cliff at the mouth of the valley. A similar even higher ridge guarded the northern approach. Having once climbed up to the ridge, walking became relatively easy again and it felt like being on a high, forested castle wall with a level surface often no more than ten feet wide. The only problem was to find a way down, but, having done so by lowering ourselves and our packs from tree to tree, we eventually reached the level floor of the valley. This was a place where even the Penan claimed never to have been before. There was a rare stillness and enchantment there where the wildlife feared man less through never having been hunted. The river ended in a deep clear pool among the rocks and boulders brought down when it ran in spate further on into the valley. I bathed there and left the men to build a good camp next to the water, before walking on down the dry river bed. It was quite unlike anywhere else in the park. With the open sky above and the towering white cliffs on either side I was able to stroll easily along a wide sandy track marking the main flood course; I was also able for once to walk silently and, whether because of this or because no one had walked there before, the sambur (*Cervus unicolor*) which I met face to face round a corner did not run away but stared back wide-eyed for a few moments. These, the largest Borneo deer, are much prized for their meat. A big one will produce about four hundredweight and no Berawan or Penan would have been able to resist trying to kill it had one been with me and armed with gun or blowpipe. Instead this female standing out bright red in the open was able to turn and vanish with one bound into the undergrowth.

I heard movement in the trees and saw a black male gibbon (*Hylobates muelleri*) hanging by one arm and leg, peering from side to side to make out what I was. Again, although there were several troops of gibbons this side of the park, most easily identified by their dawn calls and occasionally glimpsed swinging through the trees, it was rare to see one motionless. It began to make a slow series of cautious, enquiring calls, 'Wah? Wah? uwah, uwah, uwah?' starting deep and on a rising note. Then, when I made a movement, the calls accelerated rapidly to an hysterical 'Wa-Wa! WAAH WAAAH WAAAH!' as it leapt away, gathering half a dozen females and young I had not noticed.

The valley ended in a soft muddy area thoroughly rooted by wild pig where further progress of flood water was barred by a wall of limestone rubble. This was quite difficult to scramble over and from the top I could look into some of the most inhospitable terrain on earth. A series of deep, steep-sided dolines, or circular pits, in the limestone, covered in tangled and often sharply thorned vegetation, stretched away to the west, rising in a series of cliffs to the main ridge of Api. Painfully slow country to move through and totally devoid of water, this is one environment man is unlikely to interfere with and most of it remains unexplored. I could also see several very promising cave mouths in the cliffs and when I returned there a month later with our team of speleologists they were to discover some of the finest caves in the park.

Part Two

THE WORK

THE expedition was in the field for fifteen months. During that time 115 scientists came and went. They seemed to be studying everything, quite literally leaving no stone unturned in their eagerness to see, sample and understand every thing and every aspect of life in the park. In fact in most fields we were only scratching the surface because the Mulu environment was not only so incredibly rich and diverse but so little studied previously.

The most impressive common denominator of our scientists was the way each believed passionately that his own area of research was the one which mattered most. The most satisfying sound of an evening was the intense and often incomprehensible chatter as representatives of totally separate fields of study, minds which might never meet under normal circumstances, argued and found common ground and interests through their enforced contact.

Each scientist could perhaps have gone to Mulu independently and worked in isolation, though he would undoubtedly have spent a great deal more money and probably failed to achieve as much. But even more important than this was what each could bring to the general fund of information on the environment in which all were working. Botanists advising ornithologists on where and how the vegetation changed; entomologists identifying for botanists the predators of particular plants; geomorphologists and soil scientists establishing what was happening to the land and the climate on which and in which everything lived. The true value of a multi-disciplinary expedition is the unexpected spin-off arising from such meetings bringing about that desirable state of affairs in which the whole exceeds the sum of its parts. I hope that Mulu may be an example of this scientifically unlikely event being achieved.

Gathering material for this section of the book, I asked most scientists what they thought were the theoretical and practical values of their work and how they saw the future of the national park from the viewpoint of their own discipline. Many answered that they were engaged in pure academic research valuable only in so far as all additions to the fund of human knowledge are valuable. In a rich and little-known area such as Mulu, just declared a national park, it is especially important to know as much as possible about what is there and how it works if the long-term aim is to protect the region. Indeed this was our first brief from the Sarawak Government: to gather the base-line material needed for the management plan we were commissioned to prepare. But many went beyond this to point out, in some cases most forcefully, the potential wealth, other than the obvious short-term exploitation of timber and mineral resources, latent in the rain forest and still untapped, as well as the disastrous effects ill-conceived management of this fragile ecosystem would have not only on the immediate surroundings but on the whole state.

6

The Land

ABOUT twenty-five million years ago a great basin was formed between the mountains of the interior of Borneo and the coast. Granites and other igneous rocks were worn down into sedimentary rocks which were then covered by the sea. In the basin various other rocks were formed as the water rolled endlessly above. When it was turbulent, as the earth stirred under the force of unimaginable changes, sand and silt settled to become sandstones and shales. When the sea was clear and free from sediment, still and calm for millions of years, while corals and foramniferae evolved and proliferated, their shells sinking to pile up on the sea bed, the limestones were gradually laid down.

Perhaps five million years ago pressure caused the land to be uplifted, to tilt and, in places, fold over, so that huge masses of limestone and sandstone lay side by side. The waters receded during the Pleistocene and torrential rain began to fall. Since then the rain has carved valleys and created alluvial plains by eroding different rocks and washing away the silt. The limestone erodes faster than the surrounding sandstone and shale because it is soluble which is why Gunung Mulu itself is so much higher at about 8000 feet than close-by Api and Benarat at around 5500 feet, when they all started off at about the same height. Now the Gunung Mulu area presents sharp contrasts in relief and vegetation, and the contrasts are equally sharp geologically, which makes the area of immense interest.

Of all climatic regions of the earth the geomorphology of the equatorial forests is the least well-known. Until now, there have been few data about the rainfall, run-off behaviour of the rivers and relative rates of erosion of different types of rocks in these areas.

The process is continuing, and fast, since Mulu is one of the most geomorphologically active environments in the world. The rate of erosion on the limestone is exceptionally fast, up to half a millimetre a year and perhaps more. This compares with an average wearing down of limestones in England of 0.045 millimetres per year.

Ours was probably the first detailed geomorphological and hydrological study made of a very wet tropical environment and as with so much of our research it tended to raise more questions than it answered. But they are important questions upon which much depends. Understanding what is happening to the land is of vital significance, especially in a country such as Sarawak where rapid changes are being made by man to the environment.

The geomorphologists' job at Mulu was to explain the origin of the land forms. This included looking at landslides, the Pinnacles and the terraces as well as examining the limestone slopes to find out why they are so steep. They also wanted to establish the rates at which the present landscape is being worn away and in particular to compare the rate of erosion on the Mulu formation with that on the Melinau limestone. In addition to measuring the rainfall at different heights in the park they needed to investigate the sediment and dissolved material being removed by the rivers both on the surface and in the caves, and from under the soil. The programme was devised and co-ordinated by Marjorie Sweeting of Oxford University, who had the opportunity to work both at the beginning of the year and at the end. We were helped in this programme by hydrologists from the Sarawak Department of Irrigation and Drainage two of whom, Then Thiat Khiong and Lim Eng Hua, visited us during a flood period on the Melinau river.

Whether the removal of forests affects the rainfall or not is a long debated question. With the unprecedented deforestation everywhere in the tropics there is now new interest in the subject and one unquestioned fact is that moisture evaporates faster from tropical rain forests than from the scrub which follows logging. If the rainfall remains constant even for a time, therefore, deforestation must cause higher waterflow in rivers with flash floods and exceptional erosion. Once the topsoil is gone this may become massive with serious results in terms of silted-up rivers and estuaries causing navigational problems and depletion of fish stocks as well as an appalling waste of virtually irreplaceable agricultural land.

Sarawak has for many years had a good spread of rain gauges throughout the country but in common with most other equatorial countries almost none have been located in mountainous areas. This means that very little is known about how and to what extent rainfall varies with altitude, aspect and topography in tropical areas, except that it has generally been believed that the higher up you go the more it rains. In order to assess the country's water resources it is necessary to know first of all the rainfall everywhere, then to measure the run-off of the rivers and finally, by subtracting the latter from the former, the amount which evaporates from the forests can be calculated.

Also it is essential to know whether and to what degree rainfall varies locally between mountain valleys, slopes and ridges as this may be very important in explaining mechanical and ecological differences within the mountain areas.

Rory Walsh from University College, Swansea, established a set of rain gauges at different altitudes right up to the summit of Mulu. These were measured and recorded regularly by all who worked there or climbed the mountain. An interesting finding was that the rate of increase in rainfall with altitude was much smaller than expected and strikingly lower than in most other environments. The annual rainfall at an altitude of 5800 feet on Mulu was 268 inches which was only 68 inches above the 200 inches recorded at Base Camp at the foot of the mountain. In fact the lowest rainfall we recorded anywhere in the park was on the summit itself with 192 inches but this may be partly because of the wind up there which blew the rain horizontally so that some of it did not fall into the gauge. This was an important finding as it indicated that the wet moss forests at higher altitudes may be more the result of increased humidity and lower evaporation losses than of higher rainfall.

The river flow of the Melinau was also faithfully recorded through the year and this varied dramatically between the driest months of August and September when it dropped as low as 60 cubic feet per second (cusecs) and the floods in November and May when it rose to over 6000 cubic feet per second (cusecs) at times. Overnight the river at Base Camp could change from a pleasant sandy bed across which we could wade barely knee-deep to a raging torrent eighteen feet deep flooding over the banks and sweeping fallen forest giants past at frightening speed.

Rates of chemical erosion by rain and river water were measured too and were found to be very high, amongst the highest in the world, indicating the speed with which the landscape was changing, while we could all see more dramatic evidence for ourselves when the rivers changed their courses moving large boulders in the upper reaches and forming ox-bow lakes further downstream.

The crucial connection between the interests of the physical geographers, geomorphologists and hydrologists on the one hand and the botanists and zoologists on the other was provided by a major joint undertaking by the Sarawak Soils Survey team under Lim Chin Pang and Ian Baillie from the Polytechnic of North London, who had himself worked in Sarawak for some years. They mapped the complex soils of the park digging pits up to 6 feet deep all over

the place in order to describe and sample the various soil layers down to
the rock. This meant that they were among the few parties who tended to
return more heavily laden than they left since they collected more soil than
they ate food, sending their samples back to Kuching for analysis. They also
preferred to have Berawans working with them who understood about digging and who were prepared to undertake this arduous and usually grubby
toil in wet, sticky conditions, unlike the Penan who since they had no experience of agriculture found the whole exercise unfamiliar and pointless.

However, an understanding of the soils is vital both in building up a picture
of the structure of the park and in assessing the effects of future development.
Sarawak was one of the pioneers in establishing a state soil survey and in
realizing the need to base development decisions on soil knowledge. Normally these decisions concern soil changes occurring as a result of nutrient
depletion through excessive shifting cultivations as well as the erosion problems occurring both in agricultural and logging areas. In Mulu, since it is
a national park, these will not be the sorts of developments to occur, but
by creating a picture of the basic natural resources of the park and understanding the working of its overall ecosystem it will provide a useful control
against which soil changes occurring in other areas of the country being developed can be measured.

The Sarawak Soils Survey team worked mostly in the lowlands, producing
a detailed map of the intricate soils pattern found there. These alluvial and
red-yellow podzolic soils typical of lowland Sarawak were the ones with
which they were most familiar from their everyday work elsewhere in the
country and they did a huge amount of excellent work using large teams
of sometimes over twenty people at a time and tending to swamp our sub-
camps which were designed for smaller numbers. Much of the time, however,
they worked independently, disappearing into the little-visited north-west of
the park, the Medalam and Mentawai drainages.

Ian Baillie moved faster with a couple of hand-picked men digging over
forty pits up Mulu itself and in the montane areas beyond which make up
the greater part of the park. He was concerned with characterizing the altitudinal zonation of the soils rather than drawing a soils map and in putting
boundaries round the different soils which occur. Although quite a lot of
work has been done recently on the upland soils in Sarawak, the actual form
of montane soils found in Mulu had not yet been looked at in detail and
he came up with some interesting results. Mulu has generally been referred
to as being sandstone but he found that it was predominantly a clay-giving
formation, the main rock types being shales and slates. The heavy textured

soils developed there are unsuitable for the strong vertical leaching processes needed to form podsols. Further up the mountain, where the plant production outstrips plant decomposition he found layers of peat up to 6 feet deep. The way in which different soils had formed at different altitudes on the ridges and the slopes tied in nicely with what the botanists found where the mixed dipterocarp forests reached much further up the side slopes than they did on the ridge crests where the paths tended to run and so where most people went. This sort of feedback between disciplines, where comparisons between soil and plant formation on the main path up the mountain combined with meteorological results from the rain gauges, helped many other specialists, including the zoologists and botanists, to fit their findings into the general picture. It is this multi-disciplinary aspect of a large expedition, often only arising from close association in the field, which begins to justify much of the effort that goes into mounting such a large-scale operation.

Mick Day, a British geomorphologist at the University of Wisconsin-Milwaukee, also worked on Mulu looking at landslides, of which he estimated there were about 150 within the park. They occurred very frequently after heavy rain, thundering down and audible for a considerable distance. The biggest during our time there in November 1977 between Camps Two and Three left a scar which was clearly visible from the Tutoh river. Mick said he had never seen an area where there was so much evidence of slope failure so that nearly all the mountainous regions had been disturbed at one time or another. This raised interesting possibilities for further research into rates of regeneration since by the time we left, almost a year later, there had been none at all on the big one mentioned above. They also pose a potential danger for future visitors to the park as they tend to occur on the higher ridges where the paths run and the main route up Mulu passed close to and even crossed several previous landslides. With mounting use of the paths by tourists, to say nothing of the proposed road through the park, erosion would increase leading to more landslides and a greater load of silt in the rivers. Where logging occurs the problem is, of course, far greater and landslides have been documented and found to be more frequent in areas where the vegetation has been cleared. But if the object is to keep the Mulu National Park as a control, then any interference is undesirable and the whole question of the impact of future tourism which was a constantly recurring concern of all the scientists needs to be kept under continuous review. Monitoring the section of well-used path near the summit during a heavy rainstorm Mick found that some points subsided as much as 2.75 inches. This was only possible because it had been heavily walked, the surface litter had been removed and the ground had been made unstable so that wash could operate much more efficiently.

Colin Woodroffe from the University of Sheffield worked down in the peat swamps looking at the geomorphology of the interesting terraces. These are of obscure origin and range from 6 to more than 150 feet above the height of the floodplain. He surveyed profiles with a level, running at right angles to the rivers so as to cross a series of environments. The terrace sediments were deposited by rivers during the Pleistocene at a time when the base level was higher as a result of the different level of the sea with respect to the land. One important result of this work was that it provided a habitat guide based on the structure of the different lowland terrains. Thus, by identifying soil and vegetational units and relating them to the insects and other animals found in each particular habitat, land-form units could be usefully mapped and results compared. Here again Colin found it invaluable to have experts in many fields to consult on the spot so that his research had an immediate relevance. Conversely, had he been able to come out early on instead of near the end, his findings would have helped those working in other fields to identify and choose more suitable plots to study.

Most of the geomorphologists concentrated understandably on the most dramatic geological feature in the park, the vast limestone outcrop which dominated the landscape. Gunung Api at 5750 feet is the highest limestone mountain between Northern Thailand and New Guinea as well as being probably the most massive and uniform piece of limestone anywhere in the world. Those studying karst topography – how the limestone has been and is being dissolved to form these spectacular and unique mountains – argued vehemently about fundamentals. They found in the Mulu limestone an ideal opportunity for examining a relatively poorly understood subject whose conceptions have been based largely on European studies. In Europe and North America most of the limestone landscapes have been modified by glaciation within the last two million years, while Mulu is far older, having been initiated about five million years ago. Since then it has been weathered and dissolved by a combination of rainfall and rivers, high temperatures and dense vegetation but never by ice. The question is which influences have caused the particular forms of weathering found and whether the outcrops in more northern latitudes would have developed similarly in a colder climate had they not been glaciated.

Sampling and testing the water both in the caves and as it emerged from the limestone gave Martin Laverty and Hans Friederich information about what processes are taking place. Examining and collecting cave sediments for later analysis back in the UK will reveal where they came from and when they were deposited. Yap Kok Thye collected innumerable rock samples to take back to the University of Malaya to study the fauna (foramnifera) as revealed when the samples are cut into thin sections. He was particularly excited by the fact that the limestone in Mulu was up to 7000 feet thick with no break. Since there had been little change in the lithology, an unbroken succession of evolving fauna, not influenced or affected by changes in the environment, could be examined and perhaps serve as a standard time reference for the other limestone exposures in the region.

Henry Osmaston with his son Nigel, who joined us from Sulawesi having crossed to Kalimantan in a cattle boat, installed a number of small, accurately-weighed tablets of limestone to measure the weathering and chemical activity in different sites and soils. They also looked at the ways calcium and magnesium were distributed in the river waters coming off different types of landscape. Arriving early on, it was they who first tried to survey the Pinnacles and discovered Green Cave during their energetic exploration of the park.

Meanwhile Dick Ley and Roy McDonald surveyed the tower karst and the karren – the large- and small-scale surface forms of limestone affected by weathering – and argued that the influence of rivers in shaping the landscape might be much greater than previously supposed. I was impressed in my talks with the geomorphologists to hear, from their point of view, the great dangers of deforestation. One said:

The humid tropics are areas of such intense climatic activity that, despite the dense protective cover of forest, erosion of the ground is already severe. Once a slope has been stripped of its vegetation then soil erosion is rapid. This leads to base rock erosion and you get a general degrading of the slope very, very quickly. It should be understood as an energy system so that when the primary vegetation is taken out we can know what to put in its place. Monoculture is completely unjustifiable. There must be a series of layers in the canopy to intercept the rainfall and the sun's rays so that they do not strike the soil, which is very poor anyway. Everyone looks at the tropical rain forest and thinks 'what a luxurious vegetation. It must have a very rich soil'. But this is a fallacy. All the richness is in the plant life itself. The soil is usually only about 20 cm thick and often less and is soon leached. The whole nutrient cycle is a dynamic one and here the balance is very fine. If we can work out what is happening in the geomorphological and hydrological cycles then we can begin to build up a general system for tropical environments The best way to do this is to look at undisturbed nature which has found the best solution and by understanding what the balances are, try to manipulate them and model our cultural landscape on them.

Another, when I asked him what the effects would be of removing the vegetation from lowland with limestone below, such as the alluvial plain at Base Camp, replied:

A disaster! What you have overlying the limestone is not limestone-produced soil but material brought down by river from elsewhere. Limestone produces very thin soil over a very long time and here we have very pure limestone. If we erode the alluvium off the limestone and expose bare rock this area would be like Greece – bare and rocky – and it would take many lifetimes before soil built up again.

For most of us the limestone mountains were simply the most fantastic and beautiful scenery we had ever contemplated. When glimpsed through a rare gap in the trees from one of the ridges of Mulu, framed like a stage set by hanging curtains of foliage; or when watched at sunset from the *batu* above Base Camp as the sun's last rays crept up the highest crags turning green vegetation and white rocks alike to opaque purple, softening the harsh lines and making them look as innocuous and gentle as Scottish hills on a summer's evening; or viewed from far away on the rivers as we headed inland, or even occasionally from the coast itself on a clear day, when the familiar silhouette would make us stop and say, 'There's Api in the middle. Mulu behind to the right under clouds. You can see Benarat there on the left, next to the cleft of the gorge;' the eye was always drawn to the limestone by its sheer starkness and drama, the incredible steepness of all its slopes. Some sides fell vertically more than 2000 feet like the white cliffs of Dover, except that the highest point on those at Beachy Head is only 530 feet. Other slopes had trees or plants clinging to them, softening their contours so that they looked more hospitable until one came to try and climb them. Everywhere was pockmarked with dolines, deep shafts penetrating far into the heart of the mountain or shallow cockpits full of trees, between which could sometimes be glimpsed pinnacles rising into the sunlight from the rock below. Along the summit ridges the pinnacles grew larger, standing up like scales on the back of a prehistoric monster until they reached their ultimate expression at a place high above the Melinau Gorge where they rose in a great cluster, some up to 150 feet high towering above the trees to create one of the world's most spectacular limestone landscapes. To approach their bases was extraordinarily difficult, painful and dangerous, but those who succeeded said it was rather like standing in a New York street and looking up at the skyscrapers. This group of pinnacles became the expedition's symbol, stylized on our writing paper, on T-shirts and even on mugs we had made by a pottery in Miri. We built a small camp overlooking them, where after a stiff climb of some 3000 feet from Camp Five, many of us were able to spend the night and, if we were lucky, see the dramatic effects created by both sunrise and sunset as the shadows of the knife-sharp needles stretched along the side of the mountain, wisps of cloud curled over the ridge from the coast, where as darkness fell the lights of the oilfields could be seen.

The most impressive way to see the limestone mountains was from a helicopter. Time and again during the expedition when there was spare capacity on the big RMAF Sikorsky re-supplying some of the sub-camps, the crew would wave some of the members waiting hopefully at the Base Camp helipad aboard and, standing at one of the open doors, they would be able to see the whole amazing panorama pass by below. We saw wide views so seldom in our normal daily lives in the forest that the experience of having it all spread out used to go to our heads so that we laughed and pointed, sticking our faces out into the 100 mph slipstream until our eyes streamed. When our caving party first arrived from England they were fortunate enough to be taken up on their first day in camp. As they caught sight of the entrances to the underworld they were to explore during the next three months, especially the gaping mouth of one yawning hole high on Api, its rim dripping with giant stalactites like monstrous teeth, they began to bay like a pack of hounds. I recognized the feeling. When I flew on the first air drop into the park and had my first close look at the Disneyland of towers and pinnacles, precipices and peaks shining white in the sun it reminded me of mad King Ludwig's Neuschwanstein castle in Bavaria and I returned saying it was the most beautiful place on earth, more dramatic than Roraima, the origin of Conan Doyle's Lost World, more awe-inspiring than the Himalayas seen across the valleys of Nepal. Flying in a helicopter had that effect and we all tended to get carried away but the mountains were nonetheless impressive by any standards.

When we tried to climb them we found how inhospitable they were. Lacking any surface water at all, as every drop seeped away down crevices and cracks, we had to carry supplies with us or rely on the rain which never seemed to fall when we wanted it to. In fact the lush beauty of the rhododendrons, nepenthes and orchids belies the fact that droughts can occur. Run-off through the heavily eroded limestone is very rapid. There are no rivers or streams on the hillsides; the water simply disappears into a maze of passages and caverns in the heart of the mountain to reappear at the foot. Consequently the slopes become very dry during periods of low rainfall. This not only makes travel even harder since all water must be carried, but also means that much of the vegetation becomes desiccated and liable to catch fire.

The name Gunung Api means, literally 'fire mountain' and scattered fires have been reported over the years. A spectacular major fire, lasting for several weeks, was observed from Limbang in 1929, but this was probably on Benarat since that mountain has extensive barren patches near the summit ridge, which do not occur on the main ridge of Api. Local sources all testify that they saw a fire last in about 1968. We could often see from the air a burnt patch which presumably was the result of this, in a most inaccessible region on the south-western slopes of Api. Only Hans Friederich, after a difficult climb, came near to reaching this, getting within 1000 feet before being stopped by an impassable doline. He estimated it as approximately one hectare in size and felt that the fire must have been very intense as all the trees were still black after ten years. No regeneration had occurred, the only few green patches being the branches of the trees which had not died completely.

The Berawans believe that the fires are started by rocks falling and causing sparks by hitting other rocks. I do not know if this is possible but most Europeans maintain that lightning is more likely to be the cause. We always had to be very careful when making camp fires on the limestone ridges and we tried to find a flat rock or a suitable shelf, for if we built them on the matted moss and roots, even if the ground was damp, it soon caught fire and would smoulder until a hole was made through to the hollow space below.

Mark Collins, the only skilled climber among our long-term members, led each of the three main assaults we made on Api, the highest limestone mountain in Malaysia and previously unclimbed. On the first attempt a party of four Europeans including John Proctor, Harry Vallack and George Argent, a tough botanist from Edinburgh, with four Berawans hacked and clawed their way for five gruelling days up what seemed from map and visual observation the gentlest route, heading east from the Melinau crossing. The going was appalling with steeply dissected rocks, jumbled blocks, dangerous gullies and pinnacles rising forty feet from the ground with sharp edges which cut their hands. They only reached a disappointing 2900 feet before being forced to return through lack of water and time. They also found that it was impossible to camp on the broken ground of the slopes since there was seldom even the smallest flat area on which to sleep.

Mark, Harry and I next made a high-speed assault from the back of the mountain, *terra incognita*, at that stage, but Ta'ee, a Penan who hunted there, assured us that he knew how to reach the ridge and see over to the other side which sounded hopeful. Unfortunately he meant one of the steep sandstone ridges running down from Mulu to the limestone wall from which a sheer white cliff rose out of sight above us. But we were rewarded with the first view over into Hidden Valley, which we named there and then, and the seeds were sown for further exploration there. The eastern face of Api is much steeper than the western but further north, near where we had camped on our way round the mountain from Camp Five, a slight depression between the cliffs covered with vegetation seemed to provide a possible route to the top. The first sixty feet involved serious climbing with ropes up a gully which Mark graded severe to hard severe. He led the pitch using trees and spikes for protection with slings. The rest of us came up the rope bringing a few basic supplies, including some water and one camp sheet. We found that Sabang was the best and bravest climber of the Berawans with us, so he remained while the others returned to make camp at the base and to wait for us. Harry and I, who had done little or no previous rope work, found the whole experience thoroughly alarming. However, we were now into similar but much steeper country to that encountered by the first party and we were able to cut and claw our way through the soggy moss forest to an altitude of 5000 feet where we were able to camp on a tolerable site provided by a recent landslip.

Above this the going deteriorated very quickly until we were only holding ourselves on to the mountain by the rotten vegetation, whole mats of which were liable to pull away and plummet down through nearly 3000 feet of space below us. It was impossible to use ropes because of the tangled undergrowth and I have seldom been as frightened in my life. We reached 5300 feet which was only 550 feet below the summit but then decided that it was simply too dangerous to go on and dropped back to our camp to try other routes but without success.

On the third attempt Mark and John Proctor with five Berawans followed the main ridge beyond the Pinnacles Camp. With great difficulty they managed to cut a route around the Pinnacles, hacking through moss forest, edging around the sharp outcrops and balancing across deep holes. John was easing himself past one giant limestone boulder, untouched before by humans or other large animals, when it began to move and suddenly four tons of crushing rock toppled into the chasm below, very nearly taking him with it. For six days they struggled on up, their hands lacerated by razor-sharp rocks and later by tangles of slicing pandanus grass, collecting rainwater as they went and finally standing in triumph on the summit. It turned out later that a spire south of this point further along the ridge is the true summit but their efforts in cutting the first trail opened up the highest limestone formation in Borneo to subsequent scientists who were able with relative ease to reach some of the most fascinating and unusual environments within the park. The flora and fauna to be found there are in many cases quite different from those on the adjacent shale and the sandstone mountains but the single trail was so fragile and easily degraded that we had to limit very strictly numbers going there so as not to destroy the very things we wished to study.

On a subsequent botanical visit by George Argent and Clive Jermy two of the men supporting them, Inggan Nilong, our superhuman headman, and Kulat Jau, continued from the previous highest point and made the appropriately all-Berawan first ascent to the true summit on 16 April 1978. Jeremy Holloway, while trapping moths on the summit ridge a couple of weeks later, took time off to become the only expedition member to get to the very top. This too was appropriate as, although he presented a most unheroic figure for an expeditionary, being in his own words 'shy, introverted and reticent', with baggy trousers, pebble glasses and a clutter of moth traps and nets, Jeremy worked rather harder and covered rather more ground with less fuss than almost any other member.

Climbing Api for fun is not recommended as each step can be fatal and those who return look as though an attempt has been made to flay them alive. This goes for the other limestone mountains and outcrops as well. We never succeeded in climbing 5200 feet Benarat, though Sandy Evans tried from six different points but never managed to reach higher than 3000 feet. On each attempt he was stopped by sheer cliffs. He did, however, make the first circuit of the mountain and established that a skilled mountaineering team with the right equipment should be able to get to the top.

As Lord Hunt mentions in his Introduction, he and his wife took part in the first successful ascent of the twin peaks of Batu Pajing. These are prominent minor limestone peaks of about 2400 feet near Camp One which we had all often observed but thought unclimbable since the outer face presented a steep precipice. However, Mark Collins pioneered a route with Inggan, and the next day a party of eight reached the summit. Here, too, burnt patches were observed and the vegetation was particularly interesting as montane and upper montane forests were found near the summit at a far lower altitude than they occur on Mulu and Api which tower above on either side. Lord Hunt confessed he had never climbed on more dangerous rock, although the angle was only 50° at worst, making it 'no more than a scramble'. He fell heavily on the descent, cutting his hand and leg quite badly, injuries which he endured stoically during our subsequent circuit of Api, a hard walk only achieved three times during the expedition.

But the rewards of beautiful mountain flowers, dazzling rhododendrons and exotic pitcher plants and breathtaking views made it all worthwhile.

Perching high on a narrow ridge, with the sound of the rushing rivers far below carrying through the clear air, accompanied by the amplified hum of untold millions of insects, the occasional cry of a hornbill or the whoop of a gibbon, seems the perfect way to end a day. The tall cliffs and crags of still unclimbed Benarat across the gorge catch the orange evening light on one side, while far away on the other the Tutoh river curls across the flat lands to the sea; the mists begin to swirl and spiral upwards between the tortured Arthur Rackham trees bringing a welcome chill so that to crawl into a damp sleeping bag is close to heaven.

7

The Caves

As our speleological team states in an illustrated booklet* they produced on their return from the highly successful months they spent with us, 'The caves of Mulu are amazingly spectacular and provide yet another facet to the truly magnificent National Park.' From aerial photographs and previous exploration, notably by G.E. Wilford of the Malaysian Geological Survey in 1961, they had known that they were in for a treat, but what they found surpassed their wildest hopes.

Now known to contain more than thirty miles of caves, including the fabulous Clearwater system and the record-breaking proportions of Deer Cave, the Gunung Mulu National Park already ranks as one of the world's great cave regions.

During the eight months before the cavers arrived we went into a few known caves, especially Deer Cave, which the Berawan and Penan must have known about for centuries although, as far as we know, it was never used for burial purposes. Many of the smaller caves, especially in the hills near the Melinau river, had been so used but under our agreement with the Sarawak Government we had undertaken not to disturb these or to do any archaeological work. In fact we found out later that *adat* (customary law) on these matters was very strict, with severe penalties and fines even for accidentally stumbling on a burial site, while the death of anyone who deliberately disturbed or robbed a grave could be demanded. This meant that certain caves had to be put out of bounds, although this did not, as it turned out, affect the main exploration, since most of the rest of the major large caves were unknown to the local people.

Deer Cave is so named because at the entrance there are several areas of hard-packed earth where the innumerable footprints of large and small deer can be seen. These give the impression that vast herds wander in and out nightly, but in reality deer are only occasionally seen there. Quite what they visit the cave for has not been established. It is most unlikely that there is

* Brook D.B. and Waltham A.C. (eds.), *Caves of Mulu*, RGS, 1978 London.

a salt lick in such an environment and they probably come to taste the ammonia from the guano, or perhaps the attraction is simply the dry shelter. The prints are probably the result of single animals and small groups passing through the mouth of the cave over the years.

Apart from the scientific work done in this 'strong contender for the title of the largest cave passage in the world', its ease of accessibility and awe-inspiring size made it the standard first attraction for short-term visitors. Even distinguished day trippers such as the British High Commissioner and his wife (Sir Donald and Lady Hawley) and the Managing Director of Shell Sarawak (Hans Brinkhorst) with other senior government and Shell officials, who visited us from time to time by helicopter, were able to get there and back in a few hours. More than half the route follows the normal path up Mulu before branching off to the right. A confusing number of shallow or dry river beds have to be crossed as they emerge from the base of a high cliff which begins to be visible through the trees, towering up as you approach until more than half the sky above is obscured and the entrance to the cave itself becomes visible.

On entering by following a small stream which skirts a gigantic pile of debris in the cave mouth, the sheer size of the vast main chamber is hard to grasp: 570 feet wide and 400 feet high it could accommodate St Paul's Cathedral five times. It defies description. Man, reduced to feeling ant-like by standing in one of the largest enclosed spaces on earth, can only stare upwards at the distant roof, talking in whispers which echo hollowly and are lost in the vastness. Daylight floods in over the debris pile at the entrance to illuminate magnificent underground scenery, while the dark clusters of bats far above, disturbed by the intruder, whirr and squeak. Their fresh wet guano deposits give off a powerful smell here but, once crossed, the air is sweet again due to the breeze blowing through which also indicates that the passage passes right through the mountain. A fairly short scramble through semi-darkness, knee deep in mud and guano, and over giant boulders crawling with earwigs, and daylight is reached again. When we first found a way through to the somewhat smaller far entrance we were dazzled by the view. An enormous aven, or shaft, disappears 300 feet or so up into blackness and has not yet been explored. A much larger, clear stream runs into the cave mouth, before it plunges into a sump pool and disappears underground to find its own route through the mountain. Ruler-straight showers of the clearest water drop from bulbous stalactites far above and through them a mysterious green world is glimpsed past slender trees crowding the steep rubble slope which partly blocks this entrance too. Beyond is an enclosed, more or less circular valley where no one goes to hunt since it can only be reached through Deer Cave, so that it is a magical place where the wild life seems unafraid and we felt ourselves to be interlopers. Emerging quietly upstream and standing for a while at the point where the water enters the rock there is a scene from a Douanier Rousseau painting. Lianas loop between lush trees, luxuriant giant ferns cluster above the pebbles on the shore and anything is possible. Although I know that tigers almost certainly do not exist in Borneo, I always half expected at such moments to see one step out of the forest to drink; and I did see there other creatures which are normally only glimpsed. Once a troop of twenty-five grey leaf monkeys passed slowly across in front of me, the females carrying small babies clinging to their chests and stopping to look back and encourage juveniles as they leapt from tree to tree, while a couple of large males stood guard at either end of the line, watching for danger. I saw squirrels with light chestnut-red bellies and bushy tails – probably Prevost's squirrel (*Callosciurus prevostii*) – playing in the same trees and our first record of a bushy crested hornbill was also from this spot. We called it the Garden of Eden, frivolously at first, because it was an ideal place to go and escape from the activities of Base Camp, to swim and watch the life of the forest in peace. Even the fish were tame and gathered in shoals around a hand dipped in the water. It was a name that stuck.

Further up the stream, it broadened out so that we had to step carefully over and round slippery rocks and giant fallen trees. Branching off to the left, the Osmastons first found the entrance to Green Cave. They had spotted the vast overhang above it from inside the Deer Cave, but to reach it had to pioneer a very steep path up 500 feet from the valley floor. A group of us later followed their route, nearly giving up as the side of the hill became almost vertical and we had to haul ourselves up hand over hand, holding on to roots and branches. Then we came suddenly and unexpectedly to a parapet which overlooked the vast entrance cavern 200 feet wide and twice as high. Six hundred feet below, down an abrupt slope covered in ferns, *Monophyllea* and other, stunted greenery, lay the cave floor. Looking back from there the light was filtered through the foliage and reflected green everywhere off the side to give the cave its name and provide one of the most beautiful underground views in Mulu or indeed anywhere. Imagine yourself the size of a pinhead, placed at the bottom of a kaleidoscope filled with green crystals, and you will have some idea of what it felt like.

Beyond, as the darkness deepens, more wonders await. The floor of the cave is covered with a veritable garden of delicate calcite 'flowers', splash deposits from aeons of drips falling from the roof far above and creating an amazingly rich variety of cave decorations. Since these were fragile and easily destroyed by unwary clumsy feet – and also because we were tired – we rested there overwhelmed by the beauty around us. On all sides Lilliputian forests of brown and white 'trees' with delicate branches and clusters rising above smooth stems coated the rocks. Where the water fell more steadily these gathered into a great rounded stalagmite, hollow in the centre and coated in moisture which seeped down to deep canyons below where the stream now runs. Once this whole passage was probably a continuation of the Deer Cave before the section between the two caves was eroded by rivers and by collapse, forming the Garden of Eden.

I went exploring alone into the depths. It was the first time I had been by myself in such a large cave so far underground and, with only a small torch whose light could not penetrate far into the surrounding blackness, I found it a frightening and exciting experience. The going was quite easy further in and at times I was able to run along beside the stream over banks of dry mud and guano. Far from the last glimmer of daylight, round several wide corners and with the roof still far out of sight above, I stopped to listen to the silence broken only by the constant distant rush and drip of water. Giant spiders, their eyes glowing red in the torchlight, watched from the walls. A white moth fluttered into the shadows. Everything else was still, breathless, waiting. Around and above nothing but unimaginable quantities of solid rock. Although not subject to claustrophobia, I found the silence, the darkness and the solitude oppressive and the need for human companionship overpowering. I hurried back to find the others worried, for I had been away an hour, although it seemed only a few minutes.

Later I was able to go underground a few times with the professionals and found it a very different, though equally exciting business. Our cavers were a highly competent and skilled team who knew just what they were doing and took few risks. Equipped with helmets, ropes and carbide lamps they tackled each cave methodically, unravelling the complex networks of passages, blind alleys and sumps, surveying, measuring and observing so as to build up a picture not only of what was there but of how it had all come about. Between them they had a wide knowledge of most of the caves around the world, but they admitted to being staggered by what they found in Mulu.

'Just mind-blowing – they're fantastic. I've never seen so many enormous caves in one small area. It's just a caver's paradise,' said Dave Brook, research chemist at Leeds University.

Andy Eavis, under-manager of Ledstone Luck Colliery, Yorkshire, and Chairman of the Exploration Section of the Union International Spéléologique said: 'I think there's probably more volume of cave in the Gunung Mulu National Park than in any other area the same size in the world. Everywhere we've looked we've found a cave. You can literally smell them – you walk along and you smell guano; look around and there's an entrance.... We've discovered more miles of cave passage than any other expedition I've ever heard of, but that's not all; most of the passage is say 200 feet high and 150 feet wide, whereas on other trips I've been on most of the passage was say ten feet high and ten feet wide ... there are more cubic feet of limestone missing than any other expedition has ever discovered in any country.'

'What you think is a really large passage by fairly normal standards you suddenly realize is just the tip of the iceberg,' said Martin Laverty, a geochemist from Oxford, while Philip Chapman, a speleobiologist, maintained that 'The really astonishing thing is the variety of cave passages that are here. Huge shafts, very large fossil tunnels, small active streamways, big river passages – there's everything here.'

They represented an unusual combination of skills; scientists whose chief recreation was caving and potholers qualified to survey and undertake research. They had worked together many times before and their language was often incomprehensible to an outsider. Phreatic zones, vadose trenches, hading avens, dip-tubes and *arrêtes* were bandied about leaving me feeling at a loss. But their exuberance when it came to naming the more exotic underground features they discovered revealed the tremendous pleasure they so clearly derived from it all. Moulin Rouge, the Elephants' Graveyard, Sheer Delight, the Sepulchre, the Battleship, the Watchman and the Sentinel were some I never saw, but I was able to see them at work in Green Cave and to introduce them to Hidden Valley, into which I had recently cut the first path.

The first night I camped with them at the entrance to the Garden of Eden, I found Dave Brook and Ben Lyon bursting with enthusiasm over what they had found. 'Anyone who wanders about on the surface of the limestone is wasting his time,' said Ben. 'The whole story and the history of it is in the caves.' They were also a little shamefaced at having been stopped in one of the caves they had visited that day by a snake which they had met curled and ready to strike on a ledge at head height in a narrow passage. The next morning we returned there to catch it with a noose on a long pole, dropping it into a bag and sending it back to Base Camp for examination and subsequent re-release. We later saw many of these black and white snakes, some of considerable size, living deep in the caves and feeding on bats and swiftlets.

With Andy Eavis and Mike Farnworth, a plumber from Ribchester, I went into the Green Cave where, beyond the point I had reached alone, we had to rope down sixty feet and I learned to trust myself to the rope and lean out over the black space below. Mike and Andy were patient with my inefficiency, guiding me down and shouting encouragement from far above and below. We crawled through narrow cracks, dropped down into further pits, cutting the ropes to the right length on each drop to leave our escape route open, until we were deep in the bowels of the earth and I had lost all sense of direction. But they always seemed to know where they were and eventually we found a way through that looked promising. By then it was long after nightfall outside – time passes fast underground – and we had to return to the camp, retracing our route back along the cave and then hurrying through driving rain and more darkness to hot mugs of tea, rice and tinned luncheon meat. Eventually by scaling 'a very exposed face' and crossing an 'incredible' ledge over a 240 feet undescended pit they reached daylight through Green Cave far above Camp One.

Before leaving England for Borneo they had identified on air photographs a great overhang in the south wall of Hidden Valley as a likely fossil sink for the river which disappears underground close by. They were sure that there would be a major cave there and we duly found one which I had missed on my earlier reconnaissance. They called it Prediction Cave. The mouth had collapsed and we had to crawl in through a narrow entrance but it soon opened up into a huge echoing aven chamber over 200 feet high and wide where the exposed thicknesses of pebbles and clay showed how it had all been filled at some time by material washed down by the river from Mulu. Ahead, along what must have once been the river's downhill course the cave widened but the fill reached almost to the roof so that the only way forward was to crawl into what the cavers described as 'one of the most ridiculous passages under the earth'. For perhaps 400 feet the height between floor and roof is no more than two to three feet over a width of about 300 feet, so that we eased our way along like woodlice under a plank, except that we knew the rock was solid for maybe 3000 feet above us. It is a most exhausting and confusing way to travel, half crawling, half stooping, but we were rewarded by eventual escape into black space again where a remarkable flat 'road' ran along the side of a great pile of fallen rock looking as though early man had cleared a path; and yet as in nearly all the caves we knew that no human foot had trodden there before during the million or so years since they were formed. It is an eerie and subduing feeling.

Across the valley, under the summit of Api itself, there is a spot near the base of the cliff where a powerful draught blows out of a small opening, bending the ferns constantly and indicating a large cave system within. Although this is the only known entrance, so narrow that one person at a time can barely slip in feet first, the team surveyed nearly eight miles of passages within and came upon the most beautiful and varied underground decorations of all. Many are unique and, since reaching them involved climbing and caving skills of a high order, there is every chance that they will survive undamaged for many years to come. Unfortunately the desire to break off, tread on and even to write all over such fragile natural curiosities appears to be an almost irresistible human urge felt by the uninitiated of all nations, so that it is as well that one of the world's great subterranean wonderlands should be inaccessible for the time being to all except qualified professionals. One day, perhaps, walkways will be built and lights installed so that all who reach Mulu may see Wonder Cave, as this one was named, and many of the others; and this will be good, adding a unique dimension to a great national park. But first skilled guides must be trained and plans carefully drawn up so that unthinking visitors are not able to spoil or destroy the marvels they come to see. Already the impulse to record their journey has caused too many early travellers to scratch their names on convenient surfaces in the Deer Cave and, as we found, these are difficult to erase.

Deep within Wonder Cave a crystal fairyland awaits. A dazzling display of crystals, cave coral and helictites culminates in a cave lake where stalagmites form islands. Elsewhere gypsum trees, delicate calcite fans and more stalagmites reaching as high as thirty feet and sometimes glittering with crystals, were discovered.

The greatest discovery of the expedition, from the cavers' point of view, was Clearwater Cave, where they surveyed fifteen miles of passages making it the largest known outside Europe and North America. For nearly three miles a sizeable river, normally discharging 200 cubic feet per second (cusecs), but a staggering 2000 cusecs in flood, runs along a passage averaging sixty feet high and wide. This stretch could be navigated by boat to make a memorable and exciting tourist feature, easily accessible from the main stream of the Melinau river itself.

The stories the professionals told on their return from forays into their unknown world made it all sound easy. Yet their courage in the search for even more revelations impressed us all since sudden floods and rockfalls could always trap the unwary. Tony Waltham and Mike Farnworth explored the Terikan river caves under Benarat. Sometimes the only way was swimming, treading water while deciding which way to go when junctions appeared ahead and ducking under low arches no more than 4 inches above the surface where the river nearly sumped. Once they were nearly caught by a flood, although they shrugged off any real danger, saying there were high-level galleries where they could happily have sat it out for twenty-four hours or more. They were in a chamber when

We noticed water suddenly start to pour in through the roof. The stream on the floor increased in flow and changed to a turgid brown torrent. Realizing it was flooding we set off out – downstream. A few yards down, a new river was pouring out of a passage which had been dry five minutes earlier. Then there was a lake – waist-deep water – and the current. The water became too strong, but we just reached the vital junction and, now wading against a strong torrent reached the entrance. Outside it was chucking it down and previously dry forest was two feet deep in water, all swirling into the cave entrance.

Another daring exploit which I, personally, being scared of heights found particularly courageous, was undertaken by Andy Eavis. With two Berawans he hacked his way 1600 feet up the side of Api to the edge of the gaping shaft we had seen from the helicopter. Alone, he then lowered himself down a rope tied to a tree on the rim, dropping 440 feet in a free-hanging pitch to land in unstable thirty feet tall trees. Halfway down a flying snake detached itself from the wall and undulated past him to land on the far side. He continued down a further 400 feet to a point almost directly above some large avens in Clearwater Cave, a further 475 feet or more below. Having no more rope Andy then had to haul himself all the way back up again, but he believed that it should be possible to get through to the cave beneath. Many more such spectacular connections await future intrepid explorers on the slopes of Api. This most impressive pothole was aptly named Solo. In spite of all the extraordinary work they did and the exceptional amount of ground they covered, the cavers maintained at the end that the exploration potential had barely been touched and many more caves await discovery.

All the caves were formed by running water and they are very old. The oldest may have been formed as much as five million years ago, the youngest during the last 50,000 years. This gives them special interest and distinctive features. One of these is a hitherto undiscovered form of limestone weathering called photokarren. In the entrances to some caves solutional slots inclined at 45° are orientated towards the sunlight which controls plant growth on the rock. This gives an illusion that the fingers and ridges of rock are themselves all reaching for the light, as though it were a truly 'living' rock.

Over the last million or more years heavy rainfall on the limestone itself and the surface water driving down from the slopes of Mulu have eroded

18 Clive Jermy from the British Museum (Natural History), the scientific co-ordinator of the expedition

19 Walking through flooded alluvial forest

20 One of four sub-camps on the route to the summit of Mulu where scientists could stay and work

21 OPPOSITE Bats emerging from the entrance to the Deer Cave

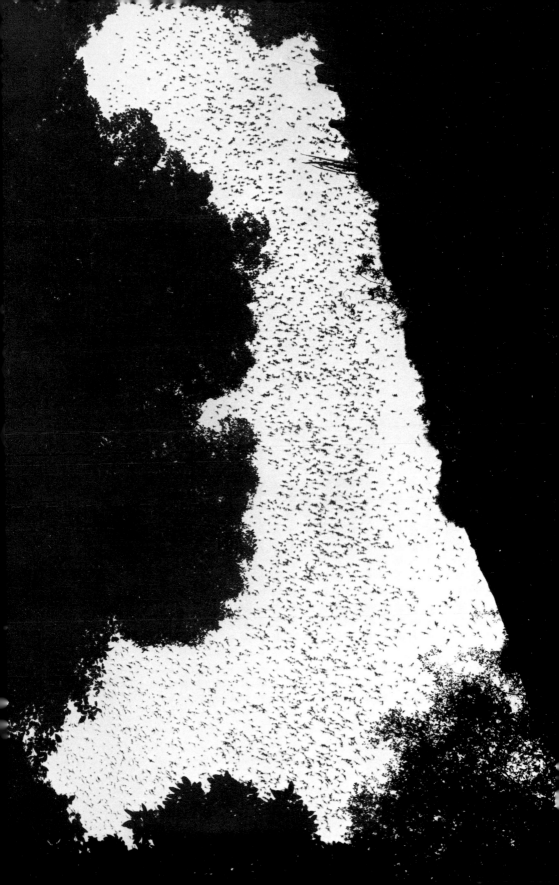

22 Stalactites and stalagmites in Clearwater Cave

23 Moulin Rouge passage in Wonder Cave

24 Clearwater Cave main passage

25 Main river passage in Clearwater Cave

26 A bat

27 Flat-headed Cat

28 Spectral Tarsier

29 Moon Rat

30 The Garden of Eden as seen from the Deer Cave

vast amounts of material, shaping the landscape outside, as well as carving cave passages along the strike of the bedding, so as to separate the great chunks of limestone into different mountains. At the same time as they became isolated so did the cave fauna and flora within them; and the super-abundance of living creatures within the caves is striking. Phil Chapman's description in *The Caves of Mulu* tells the story:

Most obvious are the cave swiftlets which roost in their tens of thousands in each of the major caves. These are not the edible-nested swiftlets of the Niah caves, but close relatives which build their nests of moss glued together with sticky saliva. Within the nest are laid two tiny white eggs which hatch into voracious chicks. Around dusk the entrance passages are filled with the sound of fluttering and clicking as the birds echo-locate their way to the remote roost after a day spent foraging for insects above the lowland forest.

In Deer Cave the swiftlets are vastly outnumbered by huge roosts of freetailed bats. On most evenings close to a million bats leave the two entrances in huge wheeling flocks or long sinuous clouds, accompanied by a great whooshing roar of thousands of pairs of wings, which can be heard two miles away at Base Camp. The acrid smell which wafts out of the cave is due to the high ammonia content of the bats' excreta, or guano. Fortunately the more unpleasant patches can be avoided by visitors, but they are actively sought out by a wide variety of less squeamish creatures such as cockroaches, beetles, flies and moths. The latter are surprising in that not only do their caterpillars eat guano and build cases of it in which they live, but the adults are repelled by light. Two of the more unusual guano bed inhabitants are long, slender centipedes which produce a bright green phosphorescent trail when annoyed, and oily-smelling giant earwigs which really belong in the roof of the cave where they graze on dead skin cells of roosting bats. Frantic to regain their lost hosts, the earwigs clamber up any available support – including passing humans.

All of these creatures are part of the complex guano bed community where each animal holds its own place in the struggle to eat and to avoid being eaten. In Deer Cave the dominant predators are very large, fast-running centipedes with extremely long legs and poison claws set below the head. As they are up to eight inches long it is fortunate that they are shy of man and run away from light. In the swiftlet-occupied caves their place is taken by fearsome huntsman spiders which manage to catch their favourite food, a type of large meaty cricket, despite the latter's early warning system – a pair of constantly waving antennae, eighteen inches long. The bats and swiftlets have their own predators, black and white striped snakes up to eight feet long, which creep up on their prey as they sleep suspended from the ceiling of the cave, or even ambush them as they fly through constricted passages.

But the animals which have really made the caves their own are small, delicate, retiring creatures found in remote passages, well away from the fierce struggle of the over-populated guano beds. Among these are minute, delicate white shrimps and isopods, eyeless white crabs, tiny blind beetles and unearthly-looking cockroaches. They form their own deep-cave community, simpler than that of the guano beds, but with similar types of animals in the key positions. The dominant predator is again a huntsman spider, but it is smaller, more fragile, creamy-white in colour and probably blind. Even so it is fearsome to its prey and is a prime example of how the animal life has adapted to the sunless environment deep within the caves of Mulu.

So much wildlife in the caves makes their exploration much more interesting, but is also adds some unexpected discomforts. Meeting large snakes underground was somehow always a little more alarming than on the surface, although the ones that lived there seemed inoffensive enough to man, either remaining still until caught or gliding off about their business. One snake I saw deep in Green Cave came across one of the lengths of white climbing rope we had left trailing down a steep slope and paused alongside it for a moment as though trying to make friends. None attacked, except when cornered. One struck out at Tony Waltham's carbide lamp while he was trying to photograph it. 'Its teeth actually clanged on the reflector!' he told me afterwards.

More alarming were the centipedes which we knew could give a vicious bite and the spiders which we were assured wouldn't but which looked very nasty. Most uncomfortable were the hairy earwigs, whose size – between $\frac{3}{4}$– 2 inches long – and sheer numbers made them hard to avoid. Often someone who had been standing still for a while, thereby giving the eagerly climbing hordes a chance to invade his whole body up a sleeve or trouser leg, would suddenly cease his scientific observations or admiration of the view with a shriek. Scratching, clutching and leaping about he would tear off his clothes and literally scrape the clinging creatures off in handfuls. Others minded less and simply ignored them. I remember someone pointing out to Sandy one evening at supper after a Deer Cave visit that he had an earwig on his neck. Removing his shirt to reveal several dozen more coating his body, he began calmly to pick them off one by one and flick them to the floor, while continuing to eat his soup with the other hand.

Thus while some might think the caves a nightmare world, we found them both beautiful and fascinating. Biologically nothing is wasted in them. The simple food chain within is a microcosm of the vastly more complex and mysterious jungle outside, the frontier bridged by the bats and swiftlets bringing in, with their droppings, the nutrients necessary to support life.

8

The Vegetation

WHEREVER there is soil in the tropics, even that poor in the nutrients needed to support life, vegetation springs up. The variety is almost endless, the diversity bewildering and the adaptations which have evolved to cope with peculiar circumstances are fascinating. Where conditions permit, the forest towers to an immense height, producing the finest timber in the world and yet often quite literally feeding on itself. Without the forests the land would be a desert. Even the life in the caves is dependent on the guano brought in by birds and bats which feed outside by day and by night.

The botanical richness of Mulu is exceptional. There are two main reasons. Firstly tropical rain forests are the richest, most complex ecosystems in the world and those in South-East Asia are the grandest, most prolific and probably the oldest of all. Whereas in the British Isles, for example, there are around thirty-five native tree species, of which most are not truly indigenous and only a handful are likely to be seen in one place, in Sarawak no one knows how many species there are although 2500 would be an informed guess. More dramatically up to 780 species of tree – over twenty times the entire British tree flora – have been counted in one ten-hectare plot. Making representative collections under these conditions is extremely difficult since the number of species increases with increasing size of the sample area.

Secondly Mulu is of particular interest because the national park contains within its boundaries most of the land types and resulting vegetation formations of Borneo, close together and over a wide altitude range.

In the valleys of the Melinau, Mentawai and Terikan rivers there is flat land on alluvial plans where, on gley soils, dense high forest with an uneven canopy grows. Emergent trees, often with massive buttresses, may reach 130 feet. In undrained hollows between low shaley ridges deep peat swamps form where the forest is sometimes stunted and open, or swampy pools may develop in deep shade while, on the banks along the winding rivers, soils freshly deposited by the water cause the trees to grow large and to overhang the river. Sandstone terraces of varying heights occur throughout the alluvial plain and on these can be found the distinctive tropical heath forest or *kerangas*. The word means, literally, that rice will not grow there on the poor podzolic soils and this lack of nutrient is indicated by the typical pole-like aspect of the many small trees, looking like saplings in a young plantation. It is an absorbing environment to which we will return in the next chapter.

On the limestone, wherever there are slopes or screes, the trees still grow to a great height in spite of the lack of humus and the fact that all water drains away fast. The undergrowth is often very dense with ferns, aroids and lianas of one kind or another. Higher up on the broken terrain of the ridges and cliffs the vegetation is more sparse and the trees are smaller and often twisted and contorted into strange shapes. Through them the fantastic white pinnacles protrude, their knife-sharp ribs bare and devoid of even the smallest plants. At the very top, woven mats of pandanus cover the limestone pillars but, wherever there is a crevice and humus, shrubs and stunted *Leptospermum* trees will still continue to grow.

The slopes of Mulu and the other mountains which occupy the whole of the southern half of the park are composed of sandstones and shales. They are less severe but still strongly dissected, with steep narrow ridges, becoming steeper with increasing altitudes and separated by many small streams in deep valleys. Below 4000 feet where the terrain is less steep grow the magnificent mixed dipterocarp forests where single trees may rise to 180 feet with rather sparse ground vegetation.

Above, after passing through a broad transitional zone, montane forest is reached. Here again the trees are stunted, their branches draped with soggy hanging sleeves of mosses. This is the typical moss forest or cloud forest where the action of cloud formations which sweep over the ridges daily and the mists which linger on the slopes play an important part in controlling the environment. Between the trees bamboos and palms, tangled and thorny, make progress difficult and slow.

Higher still, on the exposed summit ridges, which are usually no more than five to ten feet in breadth, but built out with roots and prostrate stems to give the appearance of being wider, grows scrub forest. The contorted oaks and *Leptospermum* finally cease, to leave a shrubbery of attractive rhododendrons and bilberries (*Vaccinium* spp).

From the air it all looks green and softly contoured at first and to the layman's eye one tree looks much like another from above. Much useful mapping of vegetation types, however, can be done from aerial photographs using the texture formed by the varied crowns. The 'cabbage field' effect of endless bushy tops, broken only by the occasional skeleton of one which has shed its leaves or the brilliant orange of a flowering liana which has enveloped the crown, may seem monotonous. But beneath the canopy lie even greater riches for the scientists.

The trees provide a framework and an environment within which a vast number of plants can grow. The South-East Asian rain forest is floristically the richest in the world with over 25,000 species of flowering plants alone. This may be compared with Europe which has fewer than 6000 species. On the level ground, on slopes, on bare rocks and all over the trees themselves wherever a fissure or a rough surface gives an opening, something will try to cling or grow. Over 2000 flowering plants have already been identified in Mulu and the record is far from complete, while in the fields of lichens and fungi the scientists were breaking new ground and discovering new species almost every day.

Peter Ashton from Aberdeen University was the first botanist to visit Mulu when he spent two weeks there in 1958. He was writing a book about the *Dipterocarpaceae*, the family of large rain forest trees whose giant domed crowns dominate the canopy of Far-Eastern evergreen forests. Seeing the extreme diversity of Mulu he recognized it at once as an area of potential importance to the biologist since the different habitats posed interesting questions about how nature had been able to produce such apparent luxuriance from such inhospitable and infertile soils. Through his work he discovered to his great surprise that there were many more species in the dipterocarp forest on the relatively poorer soils than there were on more fertile black soils elsewhere. This led him to consider the practical implications of regarding forested land, too steep and too poor to be suitable for agriculture, not simply as a source of timber. Instead he, like many others, became deeply concerned that through exploiting one inedible crop only we may be destroying an invaluable potential food source. In the future more and more food will be needed and the likelihood of conventional agricultural discoveries and development solving the problem is small. Every crop of world importance was already known to man a thousand years ago and hardly any new crop has been developed by Western science. As we outgrow the terrain to which we have adapted ourselves – and Borneo is a particularly good example of this, where more than half of all food is imported and people are moving into lands they have not learned to exploit – the only way to survive will be to learn how nature has succeeded and then to try, subtly, to copy her.

Once it is understood how the rain forest works, how the mantle it forms over unstable soils prevents erosion, trapping and recyling the nutrients, then it may be possible to simulate these conditions. Once the trees and other plants have been identified, experiments can be conducted into their possible uses; the valuable ones can be bred or crossed with existing cultivars; some may provide new food sources as vegetables or as basic carbohydrates and fats; others may have medicinal uses. Peter Ashton believes that research along these lines is of the utmost urgency and relevance. Before long it will be too late and gone for ever will be the opportunity for man to exploit these difficult lands on a permanent basis. Gene pools will disappear and with them the chance to improve our lamentably meagre knowledge of a vital resource. It has not yet been fully established, for example, how many trees which have reached a large enough size to flower and fruit are needed to conserve and maintain that population in perpetuity. To answer this question we need to know how far the pollen and the fruit travel, carried by insects, larger animals and the wind. Co-operation may be needed between scientists representing widely different disciplines.

The rambutan, a popular and delicious fruit related to the lychee, is only eaten in the wild by monkeys and apes. They eat the pulp around the seeds which they then spit out or swallow so that they pass through the gut. It has recently been discovered by some of Peter's Malaysian students that some wild rambutans do not germinate unless their skin and pulp have been removed by monkeys in this way. If the monkeys go, so also within one generation could go all wild rambutans, which make such a familiar sight at most Far-Eastern markets.

Likewise bats are not usually thought of as being very useful to man except, perhaps, for the guano they have produced over the years in certain caves. And yet one particular species of bat, *Eonycterus*, which is found in the caves of Mulu as well as in others near Kuala Lumpur, seems to be the exclusive pollinator of the *cultivated* durian. This most luscious and sought-after fruit, an acquired taste to some due to its powerful smell but an obsession with the majority who crave it, is thus utterly dependent on the survival of the bat. Already durians are becoming scarce and expensive in parts of west Malaysia and there seem to be two contributing causes. Firstly the limestone caves where the bats live are being quarried so that their habitat, where they roost by day, is being destroyed. Secondly, the durian is not their staple diet. It only flowers once or twice a year and the bats, nectar feeders, must have food all the time. Their main sources of food are the *Sonneratia* trees growing in the coastal mangrove swamps. This land is being reclaimed for agriculture, roads and houses. As the bats' staple diet is destroyed, so they will decline in numbers and so, too, will the durian. This is another example of how the actions of man in one direction may affect the balance of nature and indirectly man's own wellbeing in quite unexpected directions. It all goes to emphasize the need for places like the Gunung Mulu National Park where research can continue into these complex but vital subjects.

The vegetation survey of the park began when Robb Anderson made, in 1961, the first of his many trips there. Since then teams from the Forest Department, latterly under the direction of Paul Chai, forest botanist, have begun to make surveys of the different forest types. The diversity is so great that it was not possible to study them all in detail. Instead sample plots in which all the trees were identified were established in each of the vegetation types. This information formed the basis for much of the work done by the expedition's scientists. Both Robb Anderson and Paul Chai visited us regularly in the field to continue and extend the survey. Their familiarity with the terrain and its inhabitants, their experience of the workings of government and their wise advice, no less than their encyclopaedic knowledge of the botany, made them invaluable and ever-welcome members.

Twenty other botanists also took part and helped with this survey. Their interests covered such a wide field and were often so specialized that it will be impossible here to do more than touch on their work. Indeed this applies to all the members so that any reader wanting to pursue a line of research further must refer either to the monograph on Mulu published by the Sarawak Museum as a result of the expedition, or to the scientists' own published findings as they emerge.

The botanical programme set out to make a representative collection of vascular plants, bryophytes, lichens and fungi. The objects were primarily to gather material from which an inventory could be compiled and to prepare a vegetation map as background for the management plan. In addition certain specialist collections were made as well as a cytological survey of the ferns, lycopods and selaginellas.

George Argent, from the Royal Botanic Gardens, Edinburgh, was specializing in *Vaccinium* (bilberries) but extended his work to cover all *Ericaceae*, which include the very handsome rhododendrons as well. He also collected *Gesneriaceae* and *Zingiberaceae*, the African violet and ginger families, looked at wild bananas of which there are four species recorded in Mulu including one endemic, *Musa muluensis*, and did some general collecting in localities which had not been visited by other botanists. Edinburgh has had an historical interest in Mulu since two of their botanists went there in the sixties. A lot of new species were described as a result of their visit and the Gardens were keen to build on their work. With George was Ross Kerby, Assistant Curator of the Glass Department at RBG Edinburgh. He was a horticulturist, there to collect live plants, cultivate them back in the tropical glasshouses, bring them into flower if possible and so greatly extend the value of the collecting work. His presence represented something of a breakthrough since it was several years since a horticulturist and a taxonomist had travelled together. In times of financial stringency it is difficult for scientists to get into the field. Although their work seemed to me to cover a wide enough scope to justify amply their time on the expedition, both George and Ross asserted that without our organization and the cost-effectiveness of taking part in a large operation their chances of reaching Mulu would have been remote.

George visited us a second time, during which he collected as far as the false summit on Api and also made the first ascent of Gunung Mulu's neighbour, Gunung Tamashu, at 6270 feet, the second highest mountain in the park.

John Dransfield from Kew, who had spent several years previously working in Indonesia, was perhaps our most passionate botanist. His speciality is palms, on which he is a world expert, and his enthusiasm to visit Mulu was so great that he joined us only a week after he and his beautiful Indonesian wife were married. Like so many, he found it difficult to avoid superlatives when describing Mulu and stoutly maintains that it is the richest forest in the world for palms.

Despite their commercial, ethno-botanical and horticultural significance, palms are a very neglected group on which relatively little work has been done in Borneo for the last hundred years. Rattans are widely used in furniture making and wickerwork, the raw material being almost exclusively gathered in the wild. Now, as the forests vanish, some research is being undertaken into their potential for cultivation and it is urgent that the more valuable species are identified and collected before they are lost. For this a specialist is needed, since palms, which include rattans, are a difficult group. When John arrived only ten species were on the list for Mulu. By the time he left after only three weeks in the park, he had produced an inventory of 121 with more collected by Paul Chai still to be identified in Kuching. Although so rich in species, with a few exceptions they were nowhere very common and rattans in particular are usually very painful and difficult to collect due to their sharp thorns and creeping, climbing behaviour. Another problem John faced was that, even in the park, the finest rattans had usually already been gathered by the Penan and Berawans before they had had a chance to flower, so that he was only able to obtain sterile collections which are much harder to describe. This he found particularly frustrating when he was discovering so many new species and he urged us to do our best to dissuade our men from their normal practice of using rattans indiscriminately when making camp. We therefore issued quantities of cheap plastic string and insisted that this was used for all tying purposes such as fastening back packs, binding pole bridges and tying down camp sheets. It was a constant battle since the Berawans and Penan could not see that the supply of rattans was not infinite, while plastic string offended several members' aesthetic sensibilities and needed to be cleared up so as not to make litter.

Leloh, the Penan allocated to work with John, had an extraordinary knowledge of rattans, having names even for ones for which he had little or no use. He was able to identify those which were best for making the frames of *selabits*, the ubiquitous local rucksacks, while others were more suitable for doing the fine decoration work on baskets or mats. Some had good fruit but no other value, while others, notably the so-called walking stick rattan, *Calamus scipionum*, was good for trading with Chinese people who carried it by boat to the coast. He was also naturally familiar with the five species of palm from which the Penan extract sago, their staple diet, as well as those used medicinally. The most notable of the palms containing the delicious palm cabbage or 'heart of palm' was a magnificent tree, the tallest palm in the park when mature, called *Caryota no*. Sadly this was not common as, regrettably, collection of the edible core entails cutting down the tree before it flowers, so reducing the possibility of regeneration.

All this was of great value and interest to John, who believes that many of the palms should be protected internationally and has already nominated *Caryota no* for inclusion in the IUCN *Red Data Book* of threatened plant species. Another aspect of the plant flora in which he was interested was their horticultural potential. Many of the palms are very beautiful and bringing them into cultivation might help their conservation by bringing attention to them as well as ensuring that they will continue to grow domestically even after they might have become extinct in the wild.

No one country can ever have enough expertise to tackle such a large project as the one we mounted. In addition to British and Malaysian botanists, two Danes, a German, a Dutchman and an Australian joined in the forest survey. Scientists from some twenty nations will identify the material collected. Duplicates of all collections were sent to Kuching and, in addition to Paul Chai, several other officials from the Forest Department there joined us from time to time. Ben Stone came from the University of Malaya to look at *Pandanaceae* and *Rutaceae*, discovering a new species (*Pandanus microglottis*) and an as yet unidentified true citrus. Ruth Kiew from the University

Pertanian, Kuala Lumpur, came with her husband, Kiew Bong Heang, a zoologist, to make a study of the herbaceous and shrub vegetation layers in different forest types. The smaller and less conspicuous forest plants of the tropics have been less well studied. Colourful flowers like orchids and rhododendrons are relatively well known but in other groups there is still much to be found. The first stage in considering how to manage a forest is to know what is in it and this is where the specialists come in. While pursuing their own speciality most also added to the general fund of knowledge by doing general collecting work as well.

Ivan Nielsen from Aarhus was a specialist in a particular group of *Leguminosae* called *Mimosoideae*, and he only found eleven species. Yet his total collection was over 4000, being five duplicates of each of eight hundred different plants, which will help to build up a picture of the park as they are sent to other specialists for identification. The other Dane was Carlo Hansen from the Copenhagen Botanical Museum who specialized in *Melastomataceae*. He had been working on this family for eight years but had never seen any growing wild in the field, although it is one of the biggest families of flowering plants of all with some 4000 species. Most occur in the New World, and some are grown as ornamentals. He was pleased with his collection, finding some fifty species of melastomes in the park. A reflection of the strength of the Danish kroner as much, perhaps, as our own cost-effectiveness, was the surprise both Danes expressed at how cheap participation in the expedition had proved for them. Ivan told me that a couple of years before some field work he had done in Thailand had cost an average of £40 per man-day, some six times as much as being with us, without taking into account the free RAF flight.

Further down the botanical scale, diversity increases still more. Twenty-five thousand species of *Bryophytes* (mosses and liverworts) have been described and Dries Touw from Holland had a successful time in the alluvial and montane forests collecting about 1700 specimens, most of which would only later be identified by microscopic characteristics back in Leiden. Most prefer a very high atmospheric humidity which is produced on the higher slopes by the mist but in the lowlands is dependent on the enveloping protection from the sun of dense vegetation under a continuous canopy. They too will therefore die immediately if the micro-climate is changed through logging.

The taxonomic record of fungi and lichens is sparser still. Knowledge is only at the stage reached 150 years ago in the fields of trees and flowering plants. Consequently there is far more pioneering work to be done. Walter

Jülich, a German mycologist working in the Rijksherbarium at Leiden, came to study fungi, especially those living on wood and, incidentally, often destroying it. No book has ever been written on the mushrooms of South-East Asia so that he was able to start virtually from scratch, collecting an average of about 100 specimens a day, of which half were new to science. From Mulu he went on to Thailand for two months with the result that he returned to Europe with the largest collection of fungi ever made in that part of the world, a collection which will take several years to sort out but which will make an excellent basis for the book he plans to produce. Very few people have collected fungi in the tropics so that it is a fascinating field to work in, with many new species, genera and even families to be found. At the same time many of the species also exist in Europe and America so that it is essential for good taxonomy that the work is done by someone already familiar with those regions. This will also be of great value to the resident scientists continuing research on the spot. Chin Fook Hon, the Sarawak forest pathologist, who spent some time with Walter in Mulu, recognized the need for this, since he was often using generic names based on literature published more than 100 years ago and now long out of date. There is therefore a great need for new descriptions and keys, especially since there is a growing awareness of the highly destructive effect of many species of fungi on growing timber and the resultant economic value of identifying and understanding them.

Lichens in the tropics are also poorly known and they too have a potential role for conservation since they are excellent indicators of air pollution levels. Brian Coppins from the RBG Edinburgh had worked on this in England and leapt at the chance of doing pioneering research in Borneo where, apart from those on Mount Kinabalu, virtually no major collections had previously been made. Nathan Sammy, a biologist who trained at the University of Singapore and now works for Dampier Salt in Australia, pointed out the important part lichens play in that country in stabilizing the soil surface. While in the tropics they constitute only an insignificant part of the biomass and may not play a major role, they are nonetheless part of the ecosystem and therefore merit study.

Ferns were Clive Jermy's speciality. In addition to his role as scientific co-ordinator and the general botanical work he undertook during his visits to the expedition, he collected them for the British Museum (Natural History). Barbara Croxall from Cambridge who, like Clive, had been on previous expeditions throughout South-East Asia and Australasia, contributed, concentrating on her own speciality, the *Grammitidaceae*. They found Mulu exceptionally rich in ferns with five out of the seven South-East Asian endemic genera represented. About 60 per cent of the grammatids were undescribed species. Ferns also provided excellent material for the experimental cytological research being undertaken by Trevor Walker from Newcastle-upon-Tyne. This involves painstaking laboratory work examining the dividing cells of plants in order to study the behaviour of the chromosomes which may lead to fundamental changes in accepted evolutionary theory. Cytology is also revolutionizing taxonomy. Determining differences between basic chromosome numbers is a much more accurate way of assessing whether species are related to each other. This is a line of research with great potential significance both in plant breeding and in bringing into cultivation new wild species of economic value.

The botanists accordingly extended their basic taxonomic studies to include pure research as well as investigation of such things as altitudinal zonation and ecological observations. Before understanding how a tropical forest works it is necessary to find out what is there. Everything depends on the vegetation. The plants create the habitat for themselves and for all other creatures, while they constantly grow, shed leaves and die. They are living factories, converting the energy of the sun into the stuff of life itself. Examining what happens to the fallen leaves and how they are recycled within the system is a key question. But as long as the forest survives the process will continue without our help.

9

Forest Ecology – How It All Works

THE first impression of a lowland tropical rain forest is a bewildering profusion of plant and animal life: towering trees festooned with lianas and orchids, dense thickets of saplings fighting upwards in the gaps where old trees have fallen and everywhere the continuous calls of insects, frogs and birds. In fact, like all ecosystems, the forest is made up of comparatively few functional compartments. The plants (producers) use water, mineral nutrients from the soil, carbon dioxide from the air and sunlight energy to grow and maintain their tissues. The complex food web of the herbivores, their predators and parasites (consumers), from pigs to spiders, are all ultimately dependent upon the plants for their nutrients and energy. Finally all the dead plant and animal tissues are processed by the decomposers; the fungi and bacteria as well as worms, millipedes, termites and other soil animals.

Unless the nutrients are recycled through decomposition the plants would stop growing and a carpet of dead plants and mummified corpses would build up on the ground. In any forest ecosystem there is a limited quantity of mineral nutrients which has accumulated over hundreds of thousands of years. In temperate forest regions, where decomposition is slower, a higher proportion of the nutrients are in the soils in the form of humus and leaf mould so that if the forest is cut down regrowth is fast because the new trees can utilize the accumulated nutrient capital.

The great biological cycles of carbon and oxygen are also balanced to a large extent by the rain forests of the world. All consumers and decomposers use oxygen and carbon compounds to support their life processes. The carbon dioxide is re-utilized by green plants to produce new carbon compounds by photosynthesis and the oxygen in the air is replenished during this process. The plants also use oxygen to maintain their tissues but there is a net gain in oxygen from their activities to balance world oxygen consumption.

In humid tropical forests, where decomposition is usually rapid, the soils have been leached by torrential rains over thousands of years and contain only a small pool of mineral nutrients. The essential nutrients, accumulated in the forest ecosystem from soil, dust and rain over vast periods of time, are conserved by highly efficient cycling between the producers, consumers and decomposers. They are held in the plants and animals rather than in the soil. When this living cycle is broken by logging and burning, the continuing high rainfall soon washes away the dead leaves and ash leaving a stark and impoverished landscape behind. The soil is now exposed to the intense tropical sun and recolonization by plants is inhibited by the nutrient-poor soil and harsh environment. This problem is at the heart of all concern over the rapidly disappearing tropical rain forests of the world. These are well known to be the most complex biological systems to have developed on earth and yet it is astonishing that very little information is available on how they actually work.

One of the difficulties is that very different things happen in different types of tropical rain forest. In most, the plant litter decomposes so fast that the process is almost visible. The tree roots grow over and through leaves not long after they fall to trap nutrients as soon as they are released by decomposition. Fungi and bacteria are present in astounding numbers, breaking down the litter into its constituent parts and making it available to the plants. In one particle of soil the size of a sugar lump there may be as many bacteria as there are people in the world, as well as several yards of fine fungal filaments or *hyphae*. In some forest types, however, those growing on the very poorest soils, overall decomposition rates are comparatively slow and a thick deposit of organic matter has accumulated in the soil. The reasons for this striking phenomenon may be the chemical composition of the leaves and/or waterlogging of the soil. These complicated and widely differing processes generate fascinating puzzles about the composition and operation of what is called tropical rain forest, much of which in an untouched and virgin form covered the Gunung Mulu National Park.

The Forest Ecology Group (FEG) programme was designed to try and find answers to some of these questions. Mulu provided an ideal site due to the close juxtaposition of so many different undisturbed forest types. John Proctor of Stirling University, a botanist, headed the programme, spending thirteen months in Mulu. He was assisted by his wife Sue and by Harry Vallack, both of whom also stayed with us the whole time. Jo Anderson from Exeter came out twice to head up the animal and microbial side of the project and Mark Collins, another long-stay member, was seconded from the Centre of Overseas Pest Research for a year to study termites as part of the group.

Early on John Proctor and his team established one-hectare plots in each of the four main lowland forest types. These were firstly alluvial forest, perhaps the rarest and most threatened type, since virgin areas which have not previously been farmed are usually the easiest of access and therefore the first to be logged or cleared for cultivation. Indeed, even within the national park doubt was expressed over whether some of this forest had or had not been farmed by the Berawans or other races at some distant time. Although it was almost impossible to tell, simply by looking, whether some of the trees had been cut down and crops grown a hundred or more years ago, it was important to get it right. Subtle changes in the biological composition of the forest would linger at least this long and would prevent a true comparison of undisturbed natural forest types being obtained. The Berawans had oral records of settlement along much of the Melinau river and its tributaries, although the boundaries of one-time farms were not clearly known. As a result, John became convinced early on that more of the alluvial forest than originally suspected was old secondary growth. The plot they had selected within the first few weeks (Plot 1) was abandoned and a new site (Plot 1a) some forty minutes' walk from Base Camp, in an area all agreed was virgin, was marked out. Liable to flooding, infested with horseflies and mosquitoes, but otherwise rather poor in animal life, it was one of the least popular of the FEG plots. John reckoned that twenty-five per cent was added to his working time there (compared to other plots) through his having to stop and swat flies so often.

Their second plot was in the mixed dipterocarp forest just above Camp One. Here on the lower slopes of Gunung Mulu grow the largest trees in the park producing the finest potential timber. This area is the most species-rich of all the forest types with a matching diversity of animal life producing intense activity on the forest floor. Yet this was one of the most pleasant environments in Mulu to walk through. The towering trees shading the ground and inhibiting undergrowth often produced the feeling of being in a temperate beech wood, except that the ceaseless crescendo of insect noises far surpassed even the loudest English summer hum.

A third plot was on the lower limestone slopes of Gunung Api at about 1000 feet on the side of the Melinau Gorge. Few continuously wet regions in the tropics have good areas of lowland forest on limestone so that this made a valuable contrast with the other types on a site which could be reached in a few minutes from Camp Five.

Finally there was the *kerangas* plot on a sandy terrace out in the lowland plain and also not far from Camp Five. This was perhaps the most interesting forest of all, growing on a leached sandy soil that appeared depleted of nutrients. Superficially the forest looked like a forestry plantation because of the high proportion of even-sized pole-like trees although some massive trees were also present. The tree leaves were smaller than in the other forests and there seemed fewer birds, mammals and large soil animals. One hypothesis for the paucity of consumers is that the leaves are protected by high concentrations of tannins to reduce losses – to herbivores – of the trees' impoverished nutrient capital. The result of the FEG's experiments pointed to other interpretations of the phenomenon but the *kerangas* is a unique forest type containing many specialized animals and plants. These specializations are particularly directed towards capturing the potentially limited nutrients by short-circuiting or localizing the normal cycles. The ant plants, or myrmecophytes (*Myrmecodia* or *Hydnophytum*) have ants living in the tuberous base which not only swarm out to protect the plant if it is disturbed by planteating animals, but also glean the forest for insect prey which are carried back to the nest. In another myrmecophyte, *Dischidia*, the ants live in a similar manner between two leaves closely opposed like cupped hands. *Dischidia* is also found growing on the trunks of the large trees in the *kerangas* where bracket-like leaves collect detritus falling from above and form small individual compost heaps from which the plants also draw their nutrients.

The pitcher plants (nepenthes) shortcut the nutrient cycles by preying on insects directly. These most spectacular tropical plants have modified leaf tips forming deep pots of varying shapes and sizes, containing a pint or more of water. Describing one found in Borneo, the eminent Victorian botanist Sir Joseph Hooker wrote, 'A very elegant claret jug might be made of this shape.' He named it *Nephenthes Lowii* after its discoverer, the British Government official, Hugh Low. Contrary to what is often thought the lid does not quickly shut to trap insects and other small animals. Rather insects are attracted by scent and, possibly, colour to feed on the lid's glandular secretions. The lip of the pitcher is slippery and insects venturing on to its surface fall in and cannot crawl out over the projecting rim. Instead the liquid, which contains a weak enzyme solution, partly digests them so that the plant tissue absorbs the nutrients. Such a centre of water and nutrients could never remain unexploited over evolutionary time and a whole range of insects and even tadpoles have adapted to living in the soupy fluid. There is an ant which dives underwater to catch drowning prey before dragging it to the side and eating it; also a shy larva which extends a long periscope to the surface of the liquid for air. Details of the lives of these animals, including how the young frog escapes from its nursery, are unknown and would repay detailed study of this fascinating system.

The Forest Ecology Group's research involved measuring the fall of plant litter in these different forest types and estimating the rate at which it decayed on the forest floor. Leaves fall all the time in the continuous wet tropics. Some trees lose them all at once, others shed them continuously. The pattern varies but, once fallen, the leaves begin to decay through bacterial and fungal action and are broken down by soil animal-feeding activities. To catch the falling leaves the group needed litter bags which, when suspended with string between neighbouring trees, could be pulled open to achieve a catchment area of one square yard. They planned to put thirty-five of these bags in each plot, but the cost of having 140 of them specially made was going to be tremendous and so before the expedition began they looked around for a cheap solution. Fortunately Jo Anderson approached the Governor of Exeter Prison and it was agreed that, as a change from mailbags, prisoners would sew litter traps for him. The results were excellent.

The contents of each bag were collected every two weeks and then sorted laboriously into leaves, twigs, fruit and flowers and so on before each category was dried in an oven specially designed for John by technicians at Stirling University. A vital piece of equipment, it worked perfectly throughout. They were then weighed separately, probably the most time-consuming task of all, undertaken patiently and uncomplainingly back at Base Camp day after day by John's long-suffering wife Sue. In addition to weighing the leaves on sophisticated scales – accurate to 0.01 of a gramme – Sue also had to estimate the amount of herbivorous damage to each leaf on a scale of one to ten. Most of the fallen leaves had holes in them or chunks bitten out. Measuring these shortly after they had fallen into the traps illustrated the extent to which the foliage was attacked while still on the tree.

But not only leaves and flowers fall. Anyone who has slept in a forest knows that branches and whole trees crash to the ground and the small litter traps would not pick these up. So within each plot they had twenty cleared areas each of twenty-five square yards, from which they removed and weighed all the dead wood. This they did on the same areas twice more over the year, so obtaining an estimate of how much heavy wood falls annually. Finally all the accumulated dried materials were shipped back to Britain at the end for an extensive nutrient analysis.

These and other studies of the leaves were of particular interest to Lee Hua Seng, the silviculturalist in the Forest Department. The information on litter fall in natural forests will be relevant in devising different forest management techniques which will yield a good crop without destroying the sensitive nutrient balance of the forest. These plots have now been made permanent and will be monitored regularly from now on and perhaps for all time.

The rate of decomposition of the litter once it had landed on the forest floor was another important measurement, as this constitutes the main food of all the ants, termites, fungi and bacteria living there; it is part of the nutrient recyling story. One method the group experimented with was packaging some of the litter in bags made of different sized meshes and leaving them *in situ*. Those with a very fine mesh kept out everything except the spores of fungi and bacteria. Those with a very coarse mesh let in all the larger soil animals such as millipedes and woodlice. By comparing the weight loss in the two mesh sizes, some idea of the importance of the role of the litter-eating animals as well as the decomposition rates of different forest types and different leaf types was obtained.

The team also set about estimating the weight of the living material of the forest. One way of doing this is to clear fell an area, chop up all the wood and vegetation and weigh everything. This system achieves a perfect estimate but involves a huge labour force and destruction of part of the forest, both impossible prerequisites for us. However, previous researchers elsewhere had produced a set of equations by which the weight of a tree can be determined by measuring its diameter and height. To this end over 200 trees were identified and the diameter and height recorded. This exercise involved the considerable and invaluable assistance of the Sarawak Forest Department and particularly Paul Chai who performed the impressive feat of identifying over 400 species from leaves and twigs gathered at precarious heights by tree climbers. Ground level support for these and other mammoth exercises in forest documentation and measuring was given by Inggan, who worked mostly for the FEG team. He was tireless in his good humour and physically inexhaustible as he carried out duties ranging from laboratory technician to heavyweight porter. At every stage of the FEG activity he was a key figure.

Mark Collins's main job as one of the FEG team was to look at the populations of termites and the larger soil animals in the different forest types. As an entomological ecologist with experience gained on several expeditions to the tropics, he had spent the previous five years specializing in the ecology of one group of insects, the *Isoptera* or termites. Termites are one of the major insect groups in tropical soils so that his estimations of their importance in litter removal tied in well with John's work on the total litter input.

Ecological data are much more valuable if gathered over a full year and Mark was glad of the opportunity of spending twelve months in the field. On the first day after he arrived he set out to collect in the alluvial forest near Base Camp, only to be horrified to find that there were almost no termites there at all. Later he was to find plenty in other environments and at other altitudes but he became intrigued by the problem of what else could be decomposing the litter in this first area. The forest was well stocked with big trees and no accumulation of dead wood had built up on the ground, so other creatures than termites had to be removing the litter. He soon noticed that land crabs were common throughout the alluvial forest and so he decided to branch out and make a study of them. The first difficulty was to catch the crabs as they lived in small holes to which they scuttled as soon as anyone approached. Jo Anderson tried to dig them out but this proved almost impossible as the holes sank deep through tangled roots and they seemed able to dig as fast as men with spades. Mark solved the problem by sinking small buckets into the ground in a grid to make pitfall traps. During their nocturnal rambles the crabs fell into the buckets and were unable to climb out. Next morning those not previously caught and marked had a number painted on the shell before being released. In this way it was calculated that there was a significant biomass of crabs per square yard on the forest floor. The problem of determining what they ate, however, proved intractable but it is conceivable that crabs have replaced termites to a certain extent in these areas.

Mark's basic work comprised digging soil cores which he and his three Berawan helpers then had to sift through, extracting all visible small creatures. These were then put in diminutive numbered bottles and shipped home for examination at the British Museum (Natural History). In all he collected some 6000 such samples representing an average of about twenty soil cores per working day and a colossal number of animals to be looked at. Termites alone were as thick as 2000 per square yard and they were only one of the great variety of animals found. Transferring them from soil core to bottle was a time-consuming business at which the Berawans became highly skilled, responding to Mark's enthusiasm as certain sites revealed surprisingly high populations. Only once did he realize that a desire to help had led one of them to try and improve on nature. A certain day's sampling produced impossibly large quantities of a rather rare termite in some of the bottles. After Mark and I had questioned all three Berawans for some time that night, the youngest, a keen boy called Paulus, broke down and admitted that he had cut open a termites' nest at the base of a tree and added the swarming inhabitants to some of the cores. 'Doctor Mark was so sad yesterday because we only found a few insects!' was his explanation.

Termites are social insects with all the complexities and interesting behaviour traits this implies. They are a completely different type of insect from ants with which they are often confused since they have acquired many similar habits through convergent evolution. Usually a nest contains one king and queen who may live in a discrete royal cell. The eggs produced by the queen are raised by workers in cells adjoining the royal cell. Some will hatch into alates or flying termites which are potential new kings and queens. At a certain time of year and a specific time of day, when the weather conditions are just right, all these are released from the nest usually in one major swarm. When a queen settles she releases a strong smelling vapour which is powerfully attractive to the young kings who race to be the first to reach her. The young couple then drop off their wings by means of special muscles and the queen wanders off to look for a suitable nest site with the king tagging along behind. Once they have started their nest the queen may go on laying eggs for up to twenty-five years, making some termites among the longest lived of all insects. During this time, as she produces successive generations of workers and soldiers, she may become gross and misshapen with a huge abdomen attached to a tiny head, thorax and virtually useless little legs.

One of the most common of the fifty or so species of termite found in the park was *Hospitalitermes umbrinus*, so called because it shares its nest with another genus of termite, perhaps because together they are better able to defend the nest than either could alone. *Hospitalitermes* and a near relative *Longipeditermes*, which means 'the long-foot termite', were easily seen because they formed foraging trails out in the open. Long columns of *Hospitalitermes* wound over the ground and right up trees covering as much as 1000 feet in search of lichens. These they shaped into little balls which they then carried home clasped in their mandibles. Some were occasionally intercepted by Mark who relieved them of their loads which he then passed to our visiting lichenologist for identification. The soldiers of both these genera had elongated snouts containing a gland at the tip from which they could squirt a sticky irritating substance. As the workers hurried up and down like heavy traffic on a four-lane motorway, the soldiers were flanking the column ready to ward off attacks by predatory ants.

Other species which feed on dead wood build subterranean structures out of their faeces on which a fungus grows, producing fruiting bodies high in nitrogen. These are fed to the larvae which need nitrogen for rapid growth. So timber on the forest floor is efficiently and quickly converted into termite bodies. Under natural conditions termites can be seen to play a vital part in decomposing and recycling the nutrients. But where cultivation is taking place they can be a serious pest, damaging crops, standing timber and buildings. Mark was able to visit some logged areas in Sarawak to make comparisons between virgin forest, selectively felled areas and areas which had been completely cleared for rice planting. In each he found progressively reduced numbers of species of termites. Certain species, however, are pre-adapted to survival in these new conditions and it is these that survive and become pests.

Higher up Gunung Mulu Mark set up ten further plots as part of the overall altitudinal zonation study. These followed an excellent survey of the vegetation undertaken before the expedition by Peter Martin, a VSO volunteer who had been attached to the Sarawak Forest Department. They also tied in with Ian Baillie's soils survey work and the geomorphologists' series of rain gauges. He found that up the mountain termites tended to disappear and other groups to take their place. Around Camp Three at 4000 feet beetle larvae and earthworms were specially prevalent. Near the top he collected some specimens of particularly nasty looking creatures, predatory leeches up to seven inches long which fed on worms and beetle larvae though they do not apparently attack humans. John Proctor also extended his litter collection into these regions, adding more valuable information to a pioneering form of multi-disciplinary research into the amazing changes which occur under neighbouring but very different conditions.

John Lewis, specializing in centipedes and millipedes, and so properly called a myriapodologist, added yet another dimension to the Forest Ecology Group's research. Centipedes are carnivores and the larger ones – up to about eight inches – can give an extremely painful bite, as Wilma Lloyd Smith found out. Centipedes are among the most important soil predators and were relatively common in much of the park. In Deer Cave they were particularly plentiful, hunting fly larvae and other invertebrates in the guano and some becoming luminous when disturbed. John's happiness as he crawled in pursuit, popping centipedes into collecting bottles as fast as he could catch them, oblivious of the earwigs, cockroaches and spiders which swarmed over his body, epitomized for all of us who watched, and sometimes gingerly helped, the dedication of the true scientist.

Millipedes are largely herbivorous, processing enormous amounts of leaf litter and humus as they trundle harmlessly along, the bigger ones looking like brightly coloured red and black toy trains. Ironically, however, they pose more of a potential threat to man, since in a few parts of the world they have become major pests, attacking cultivated crops which they devour with equal gusto.

The forest ecologists' eclectic interests really bridged the gap between the various scientific disciplines. Their awareness of the dynamic effects of what was happening in the forests, the close interrelation and interdependence of all living things with each other and with their environment, appeared to make them compulsive all-rounders. John Proctor, the only one of us to learn Berawan, produced the first dictionary of their language, a paper on their history and settlements and the definitive list of Berawan, Malay and English place names within the park.

Mark Collins made exceptionally good friends with all the local girls, became our best *ngajat* dancer, made all the mountaineering attempts and travelled widely in Sarawak and Sabah.

Jo Anderson, man of all parts *par excellence*, was tireless during his all-too-brief stays. With his bushy red beard he looked far more like the game-keeper he once was than a university lecturer. Nonchalantly holding a scorpion by the sting he would expound on its breeding habits before switching roles from scientist to general handyman.

All who came to Mulu were, I believe, conscious of being highly privileged to have the rain forest revealed to them by such stimulating companions. But perhaps the most eccentric and entertaining of all FEGs was the first to arrive and leave, Mike Singer, English but based at the University of Texas. Peering through his thick round glasses, he was usually to be seen bent over a new bush examining and muttering at its diverse insect population, which most would pass by unseen. In the laboratory he kept a weird menagerie of caterpillars, insects and eggs that might hatch into anything, and all fed on revolting rotten fruit scrounged from the kitchen. If taken unawares, he could be observed there talking to himself or discussing with his pets their likely futures in the wild or in bottles, occasionally delivering a wild gibbon hoot for no apparent reason. When entering Sarawak, a customs officer asked him, 'Your name Singer? Can you sing?' Mike said, 'No, but I can hoot' – and did so in front of an amazed audience! An articulate and funny raconteur, he was always ready to break off and tell his audience far-fetched stories illustrating odd relationships and symbioses between plants and insects.

Mike's special interest was to look at insect predators of tree seedlings, how they found their food and how much effect they had; how they camouflaged themselves and the extent to which they specialized on a particular plant. He found an abundance of aphids in Mulu, well known of course as pests. They themselves had predators which could be useful as a biological control.

For most of us the quantities of dazzling butterflies and moths provided a purely aesthetic pleasure, bringing flashes of extravagant and unexpected colour into the darkest corners of the forest. Mike was concerned with their role in the ecosystem as pollinators and feeders, asserting that without them the place would not only be less beautiful but radically different, since other creatures would rapidly occupy their niches. He and Peter Wedlake, a young schoolteacher who came out to help build the laboratory and longhouse, undertook a butterfly population study. They caught and marked and released about fifty a day at the same site, but found that they were re-catching a remarkably low proportion of those already marked. One possible reason for this could have been that the butterflies were responding to being caught by changing their behaviour so as not to get caught again. If proved this could be a significant finding. It is well known that vertebrates caught in traps are affected by the experience. Indeed in some documented cases, as with mice caught in cages baited with peanut butter, it has been found that they return again and again, presumably reckoning the taste worth the unpleasantness. But this was not generally believed to apply to invertebrates. Attempting to resolve the problem led to one of the more memorable views of a scientist at work. On the little beach opposite, Mike would lie at full stretch, inching his way imperceptibly towards a patch of sand on which he had previously urinated and to which a swarm of butterflies was irresistibly attracted. Extended in his right hand was a felt pen with which he hoped to mark their wings without them noticing. Such is the stuff of pure research in the field.

10

Mammals and Birds

THE Asian two-horned or Sumatran rhinoceros and the orangutan are totally protected in Sarawak, but neither of them is to be found in Mulu. Indeed both of these large and attractive mammals are now sadly rare and threatened with extinction throughout most of Borneo. Sightings of rhinoceros have been very infrequent since the Second World War with only single specimens being recorded every few years. No more than a handful may remain on the island, where they have been hunted ruthlessly for their horns, which are much prized by the Chinese for their supposed medicinal properties. Once they must have been quite common in Mulu. On remote sandstone ridges we often came across pools which the Berawans assured us had been dug as wallows by these splendid herbivores. Some had steep channels running into the water down which I was told the animals used to slide, conjuring up memories of Kipling's *Just So* story about itchy cake crumbs under the skin. The last rhinoceros hunted on Mulu was reputed to be the one Inggan's grandfather, Aban Inggan (Tama Nilong), pursued up the mountain, incidentally making the path Edward Shackleton was to follow in 1932, before he killed it on Gunung Tamashu, which means 'rhinoceros' in Berawan.

Orangutan may have never occupied the various habitats occurring in the national park, since the local people had no memory of them. Banteng on the other hand, the magnificent wild cattle, did roam there in small herds until fairly recently and it has been suggested that they might make suitable candidates for re-introduction into the park. Once, when I was walking between Long Berar and Camp Five, Usang pointed out a spot where in 1957, unarmed, he had watched five adult banteng pass by. Now that many Berawans and even some Penan have guns they would stand little chance of survival unless official protection is provided.

Elephants are found only in parts of Sabah and northern East Kalimantan and there is doubt as to whether they are indigenous or were introduced from Sumatra in the distant past by one of the Sultans. In one sense the absence of these and the other larger mammals from the Gunung Mulu National

Park would seem to diminish its value. The familiar concept in many people's minds of a national park derives from the great parks of Africa, where huge herds of animals can be seen grazing and lions can be approached in the safety of cars. But tropical rain forest national parks can never be like this. The forest is so dense that views, even over the treetops, are few, while the animals are always hidden in the foliage, to be glimpsed only rarely through luck or great patience. Yet, as with all other life in Mulu, the diversity of animals is immense and representative of this region of Borneo.

Mammals are the most elusive creatures to study under these conditions. Although all sightings were recorded in a log maintained at Base Camp and several specialists attempted to assess numbers through cage trapping, radio tracking and observation of footprints, there is still a great deal of work to be done before full species lists can be made. The clouded leopard (*Neofilis nebulosa*), for instance, largest of the Borneo cats and only a little smaller than a panther, was never positively sighted during the expedition. Near Hidden Valley I glimpsed a large cat moving fast through the undergrowth and the Berawans with me insisted that it was a clouded leopard (*Maci* in Berawan) but they were ever prone to exaggeration in these matters. At Base Camp there was much excitement when, on several successive nights, a marauding animal disturbed the chickens under the men's house and one who saw it by torchlight swore it was a leopard. When eventually trapped it proved to be a civet. Not far outside the northern boundary of the park, David Labang and I found the stretched skin of a clouded leopard in the longhouse at Long Medalam on the Limbang river, which the Penghulu admitted to shooting a few months earlier. David informed him that it, too, was a protected animal in Sarawak and he promised to kill no more although the skins are much prized.

The most common large mammals in the park were pigs. The species found in Borneo is the bearded pig (*Sus barbatus*). The young are stripy; the adults black, although they often appear russet red from the soil in which they wallow, and the old males are white. Traces of pig were found at almost all altitudes and many were seen or heard. They are reputed to migrate in large numbers occasionally when they may be killed easily as they cross wide rivers, but this never happened while we were there and numbers may be reducing due to hunting. The most I saw was a family of ten, including young ones, setting out to swim the Tutoh near the junction of the Melinau, which turned back and scrambled up the bank as I went past in the jet boat. I also had some splendid sightings early on of fat white hams trotting away from the previously little-used paths in the park, but they seemed to become more shy with increased traffic and would normally lie up by day in any case. The settled Penan of Long Iman use dogs to hunt them keenly as their main source of protein and, characteristically, keep the lower jaws of all the animals they kill and eat hanging in the rafters. Gathorne Medway (then Lord Medway, now the Earl of Cranbrook) and David Labang collected a great many of these which they aged and sexed before sending them to Kuching, so that they were able to assess the impact Penan were having on their numbers. A few were very young (under six months), the rest were adult pigs ranging from two to over twelve years old. It seems that young pigs between six months and two years old will keep running when hunted but the older ones turn at bay to the dogs and so can be speared when the hunters catch up. Both Gathorne and David, who had worked together in the field many times before, were invaluable experts to have with us. Gathorne, author of *Mammals of Burneo* and *Wild Mammals of Malaya*, headed our zoological programme, joining us at the outset to set up the long-term projects and later co-ordinating results from England as a member of our committee. His energy and encyclopaedic knowledge of both mammals and birds made him a formidable companion as well as an invaluable mentor. On one occasion he returned from a visit to the Deer Cave with a dead bat of a species he had not seen before. Momentarily forgetting his unchallenged status as an expert on these, I enquired innocently if it might be a new discovery, only to be put firmly in my proper place when he replied with justifiable confidence, 'If it's new to me, it's new to Borneo.'

David Labang spent about four out of every ten weeks with us during the year. In addition to his many other inestimable roles which I have touched on elsewhere, he set up in the alluvial forest a grid of wire-cage rat traps in order to sample the smaller terrestrial mammals. He and his team placed the traps on the ground, on fallen logs and on the lower branches of trees. These were baited with banana, coconut flesh and tapioca root and their positions changed when necessary. A survey of this sort takes patience, since on average only one cage in fifty would capture anything. Mammals trapped were lightly anaesthetized with ether, then sexed, measured, weighed and individually marked by having a toe clipped. After reviving they were released close to the point of capture. Rats, the commonest catch, of which five species were identified, would often come back again and again. This, however, was not a disadvantage because from the proportion of marked animals the size of the population could be worked out.

Some squirrels and tree shrews were also caught in this way but many more mammal species were recorded in the park by observation. Among the larger were the three kinds of deer. Under the Park Charter all of these, with the pigs, are allowed to be hunted inside the park by the Penan. The Berawans and occupants of the other longhouses near the park may also hunt them within certain river catchments. The biggest are the imposing sambur or *rusa* (*Cervus unicolor*) which stand four feet at the shoulder. Reddish brown, with fine antlers, the males are reminiscent of the red deer of Scotland, except that sambur only have a maximum of three 'points'. They are much sought after for the large quantity of excellent meat they yield. Understandably perhaps they were scarce and shy but we often came across their distinctively large hoofprints dwarfing all others. The barking deer or *muntjac* (*Muntiacus*) was more often heard than seen. The sound produced by blowing across a leaf or blade of grass is a well-known trick for attracting them, although it is not a bit like the deer's bark. Our men often tried this but I never saw one fall for the trick.

There are two species of the little mouse deer or chevrotains, *Tragulus javanicus*, called *pelanduk* in Malay and *T. napu*, called *napuh* in Malay. They are the smallest of all the hoofed animals and not true deer (*Cervidae*) at all. The larger looks like a big hare as it runs away, while the smaller stand only about 8 inches high. An enchanting young one barely four inches tall was caught and brought to us at Base Camp where Sandy attempted to rear it on a bottle. It became quite tame, trotting over the planks behind him on spindly little legs like pencils, but sadly died one night without appearing to sicken.

Among the more familiar mammals to be both seen and heard were the monkeys and gibbons. Andrew Mitchell carried out a preliminary primate survey of the park, observing numbers and distribution in relation to different types of forest. He also made recordings of calls which can be converted into audio spectrograms, a new tool for classifying them. In some cases certain species of primate have very few visible differences between them but by comparing their voice patterns electronically produced on paper it may prove possible to determine more easily the differences between species and also learn something of their evolution. He found increasing numbers of primates further up the mountain and this was probably due to the effect of hunting in the lowlands. Gibbons were even sighted as high as 5500 feet on Mount Mulu.

Five species of monkey were recorded in the park. The pig tailed (*Macaca nemestrina*) and long tailed (*M. fascicularis*) macaques, both of which were often to be seen kept as pets in the longhouses, will eat almost anything, which makes them easy to rear in captivity. Those kept by the Penan are said to be released again into the wild on reaching maturity. Although this seems unlikely we were assured it was so and while chained adults were a common sight elsewhere we never saw any larger than babies in Penan settlements. The leaf monkeys or langurs eat only leaves and were generally more shy, since they are hunted with special energy, having sometimes valuable gall stones (*bezoar*) which can be sold to the Chinese for enormous sums. The silvered leaf monkey (*Presbytis cristata*) is probably the rarest monkey in the park and was seen only occasionally. The maroon leaf monkey (*Presbytis rubicunda*) was the more easily seen, especially up at the Pinnacles on Gunung Api, where a group shrieked at me one night for an hour from their inaccessible fortress, the sun catching their bright orange hair.

The grey leaf monkey (*Presbytis hosei*) is less well-known and there was some doubt as to whether two species might not exist, one restricted to high ground. Andrew found them most common and easiest to observe in the mixed dipterocarp forest at Camp Two, where they were less afraid of man and soon became used to his presence as he sat still for hours on end watching and recording their calls. When Nyapun, the first of the nomadic Penan to show himself at Base Camp, arrived Gathorne Medway was there. In order to solve the problem of the true identity it was essential to examine an adult female grey leaf monkey from the lowlands. Showing Nyapun a picture of the monkey and explaining his precise requirements he said he would be in Camp Five in four days' time and if Nyapun was shooting for his family, he would like to see a freshly killed specimen. Remarkably Nyapun, who returned to his own camp near the Brunei border inbetween, arrived at the appointed time with exactly what was wanted. He had selected from a shy and elusive troop and shot with his blowpipe a perfect mature female – a feat which even the Berawans, let alone modern man armed with the most sophisticated weapon, would find virtually impossible. David Labang, who spent some time with Penan groups watching them hunt, said that they were aware of how many monkeys were in each troop and chose to leave it in peace when numbers dropped below about twenty so that they would have a chance to breed again. If so, this implies a high level of awareness of sound conservation principles but may be offset in the future by increasing hunting pressure on the food resources of the park as further Penan move in.

Philip Leworthy took time off from his mechanical repairs leaving Nigel and me to wrestle with breakdowns of outboards and generators, while he followed up some of Andrew's work on gibbons. Camping with one Penan on a ridge above Hidden Valley he watched and listened, to confirm that most of the observable gibbons in the park live on the slopes between Mulu and Tamashu. He estimated half a dozen groups each comprising four to five members. The gibbons (*Hylobates muelleri*) are the most attractive and audible of the park's primates. Apes not monkeys, they have no tails, and swing rapidly from tree to tree using their long arms. Both males and females have different calls and their loud musical note can be heard over great distances, giving an inflated impression of their numbers. Andrew found that males and females called at different times of day, the former beginning just before dawn and ending at about 7 am, whilst the females' long 'great calls' occurred about an hour later. The purpose of this time difference is unclear but certainly the early morning calls of these enchanting creatures were one of the most familiar and appealing sounds of the forest.

There is only one species of bear in Borneo, the sun bear (*Helarctos malayanus*). It is the smallest bear of all and seldom seen, but much feared. Black with a white mark on the chest, it has powerful long claws used to tear open trees in its search for honey or grubs. Sometimes they could be heard growling angrily near the path and once Nigel, cutting his way down a new route between the summit of Mulu and the Melinau Gorge with four men, had to make a wide detour when two adults barred their route. Fresh tracks were also seen near Base Camp and high on the ridge trail near Camp Four but they generally kept well away from us.

Much could be learned about the mammals from their tracks and droppings. Margaret Wise, helped by Lang, our most skilful Berawan tracker, covered sections of six river systems and found signs suggesting a widespread occurrence of at least two sorts of otters, although these shy mammals were rarely seen, and were therefore previously thought to be uncommon in the park. Once again the best sighting was from the jet boat when we surprised a party of seven in mid-stream on the Tutoh. We stopped the boat and drifted with the current as they dived, then popped their heads up one by one all around to stare for a startled moment before diving again. Eventually they made for the shore and loped off across a wide gravel bank giving us a fine view. These were almost certainly the oriental small-clawed otter (*Amblonyx cinerea*). The larger species was probably the smooth otter (*Lutra perspicillata*) but it has not yet been established whether the hairy-nosed otter (*Lutra sumatrana*) may be found there as well. There seems to be a fairly high density of otters on all the lowland rivers though they are wary of man and occasionally killed by both the Penan and the Berawans when they interfere with their fish traps.

Margaret's main study was to work with David Macdonald from the Animal Behaviour Research Group at Oxford in experimental work on radio tracking. David had been working for five years in this novel field examining the behavioural ecology of foxes, jackals, hyenas and wolves. Through attaching miniature transistorized radio-collars to some of these animals it had been found that their social behaviour was far more complex than had been previously thought. In addition to the useful scientific results obtainable from this new method of following animals, it has wide implications from a conservation point of view, since by understanding more about an animal's behaviour in the wild, better arrangements can be made both for its protection in national parks and for reducing the damage it does when its interests conflict with those of man. The technique had only been applied to a small number of mammals in tropical rain-forest areas before and doubts were cast on its viability in dense jungle with a high humidity.

The first difficulty was to catch suitable animals. The otters were too clever to get caught in fish traps set for this purpose but two Malay civets (*Viverra tangalunga*) were caught scavenging near Base Camp. These are the largest of the several species of civets found in the park, fairly common in the alluvial forest and mainly ground-dwelling. They live on a mixed diet of frogs, lizards and small insects and also eat vegetation and fruit. To attach the collar, David Giles, our resident doctor of the time, anaesthetized the animal by putting a plastic bag over its small wire cage and inserting a pad soaked in ether. Civets have quite impressive teeth and it needed careful judgement to induce a level of unconsciousness deep enough to give time for measurements to be taken without causing damage. Once fitted with its collar the civet could be released, to be followed night after night by David or Margaret holding up the receiver's antenna at different angles so as to judge from the loudness of the recurrent bleeps where and how far away it was. They found that using a 6-volt spotlight shrouded in celluloid, of which the civet seemed unaware, they could track it on its nocturnal hunting routes, which tended to follow a regular pattern. Most nights it used to pass between Base Camp and the river around midnight and had probably been doing so since the beginning of the expedition so that, alerted by the rising pitch of the receiver, we were able to gather on the balcony of the longhouse and watch its progress. It would suddenly pounce on a grasshopper then pause to munch it audibly, undisturbed by its often far from silent audience. Observing an animal in the wild close to is always exciting but I was impressed one night when David, seeing it had just stopped and apparently scent-marked a small bush, dashed down the steps to bury his face in the leaves in order to sample the aroma.

Each day the experimenters also attempted to find the civet's sleeping places. These changed regularly, being mostly in caves on the limestone and sometimes up trees. After a couple of months the batteries in the transmitter began to run down. Managing to trap the civet again, we removed the collar to ensure that it was not a lifelong encumbrance and then released the animal once more into the wild.

Many observations were the result of chance encounters by scientists going about their daily or nightly work. Night was certainly the best time for observing mammals and we would all I think have liked to spend more time tramping the paths armed with a powerful torch. But when in sub-camps we were usually too tired to sally forth again and somehow at Base Camp there was usually too much to do in the evenings. Those whose work did take them out at night were well rewarded. Barking deer were watched several times and seemed little disturbed by lights, which does not bode well for their survival as powerful electric torches become available to hunters. The moon rat (*Echinosorex gymnurus*), largest of all the shrews, shows up well at night, being white with a pink tail and snout. It gives off a foul musky smell and may be conspicuous to warn predators that it is inedible and best left alone. Porcupines (*Hysterix* or *Trichys*) were fairly common too, busily grubbing about, oblivious to their surroundings, secure in the protection of their quills. One was seen early on, heading down a well-beaten track leading towards the newly built Base Camp. Within yards of the house it stopped, looked up at the lighted windows, seemed to think for a time, then turned and trudged back the way it had come in search of less disturbed feeding grounds.

It was noticeable that most animals kept well away from man and future tourists are unlikely to see much of the larger wildlife. We allowed no hunting by the men while they were working for us, although as part of the pig survey certain people were given permission to kill one of these from time to time. Before adding usefully to our diet, the dead pig was always examined for parasites and measurements were taken of its body and internal organs. But even the most skilled hunter returned empty-handed more often than not, and they had to travel further afield as time passed, indicating that pigs, too, were giving our camp a wide berth.

The most frequently seen mammals of all were unquestionably bats. Vast numbers of free-tailed bats roosted in Deer Cave and could be seen most evenings pouring out from the entrances making a rushing noise like a sudden wind. Then, bunching together in dense flocks, they would wheel and spiral high into the sky, creating strange shapes like giant smoke rings and vortexes, drifting fast towards the south and west. This may be a peculiar defensive strategy against the bat hawks which wait nightly for their prey, although it is far from certain as other bat species do it without being specialized. The sound of the bats' wings as they flew high over Base Camp was audible above the evening chatter of cicadas and drew us irresistibly time after time out of doors to gaze at the amazing spectacle passing overhead. It must remain one of the most impressive memories we will all retain of Mulu.

Sue Proctor tried to count the bats in various ways. From the *batu* above Base Camp on a clear evening the flights from both ends of the Deep Cave could be watched through field-glasses. By guessing the numbers in one flock and then counting the flocks as they emerged a rough estimate could be arrived at. She also had a camp at the main entrance where by photographing and timing the main exodus a more accurate figure could be obtained, but covering both exits at once was difficult. The total figure is probably several hundreds of thousands but a further obstacle to achieving accuracy was that some nights when everything had been set up to count them, the bats simply failed to emerge at all. She also put up small tables covered in silver foil under the main roof of the cave to monitor the amount of guano falling on them but the teeming insect life of the cave floor tended to get there first and eat it. In the mornings, as the cave swiftlets clicked their way out into the daylight, the bats trickled back singly and in smaller groups, dropping down from great heights to return to their roosts.

While it was difficult in the time available to be confident of having produced a complete species list of the mammals of the park and quite impossible for the lesser creatures such as insects, birds are much more easy to see and identify. A dozen ornithologists took part, recording 262 species.

This total included about two thirds of all resident Borneo species; if coastal birds and those associated with man-modified habitats are excluded the proportion would be as high as eighty per cent.

Although the park is thus very rich in birds, observing them in the forest depths and treetops is often difficult and, in compiling an inventory of the species, many techniques were used to assist identification.

The observation post on the *batu* above Base Camp commanded a splendid view over the forest canopy and many of the characteristic tree-top birds were readily seen from this vantage point and well over 100 species were recorded from there.

In the dense forests many birds communicate largely by voice and inevitably much of the ornithologists' work is based on identification of birds by their calls. Tape recorders were widely used to record relevant or interesting sounds and, in some cases, to attract shy species by playing their just-recorded call back to them!

31 Black and white snake

32 Malay Civet

33 The nymph of a Flatid Bug camouflages itself as a bird dropping

34 The fruit of a *Dillenia* tree; the seeds are bright red

35 Dr David Giles treating a Penan family

36 David Labang of the National Parks and Wildlife Section in Kuchung greeting a Penan
elder

37 Penan child with
   hunting dogs gazing at
   the first white man she
   had ever seen – the
   author

38 Nyapun and his family
   moving through the
   forest

39 Nyapun's young wife

40 Seng, the headman of
Nyapun's family

41 Penan mother and children. The baby is suspended in a *selabit* (rucksack)

42 Penan *sulap* (house) made from palm leaves

43 Nyapun at a Long Pala party playing a *kelore* made from a gourd and thin bamboos; the plastic mug on the end is supposed to help the tone

44 A Penan farewell gathering at Long Pala

45 Tingang with his blow-pipe and dart-holder

Extensive mist-netting programmes were carried out in all habitats and in addition to their importance in censusing (providing estimates of relative abundance, both between species and habitats) and identification, a number of skulking birds of ground and undergrowth were recorded only by being caught in these nets.

Thus sight, sound and trapping all contributed to various aspects of census and identification work and much information was accumulated on the density and abundance of species.

The lowland forest was much the richest with a dramatic drop in numbers of species further up the mountain. As few as fifty species were recorded above Camp Four. Several projects concentrated on the bird communities in particular habitats.

David Labang had rows of mist-nets adjoining his mammal trapping area, which he opened for four consecutive days during each of his visits. By concentrating, over the year, on one site and ringing all birds captured in addition to the other routine observations he was able to assess the density of birds per hectare.

Our Canadian resident ornithologist, Kevin McCormick, lived for a year at Camp One doing a community study of the birds there. This involved looking at the division of available resources between the 108 species he found at that altitude. Fruit, insects and nectar are only present in a limited quantity and the birds have to compete for them. It is a basic biological principle that co-existing species cannot have exactly the same ecological requirements. While some overlap is tolerated between species, close observation over a long period can reveal fairly accurately the niche occupied by each. Some birds feed on the ground, others on the lower vegetation, still others in the canopy. There are those which catch flying insects, those which pick them off the trunks of trees and those which eat fruit of varying sizes. By measuring these and other parameters over a long period in a particular type of undisturbed forest, a useful baseline can be built up for detailed comparison with similar terrain after it has been logged. Indeed, without hard facts such as these it may be difficult to argue with those who suggest that selective removal of timber does little harm to the wildlife.

Complementing this detailed study of a single site David Wells led a team from the University of Malaya studying population densities of birds in different vegetation types. With Chris and Sandra Hails over a period of five and a half weeks some 700 individual birds were caught in mist-nets and examined before being released.

They found striking contrasts between the well-populated lowland alluvial forest and the impoverished peat swamp and *kerangas* areas. Some of the reduction in species on ascending the mountain they attributed to the openness of understorey vegetation on the steep slopes and consequent lack of understorey birds.

John Croxall, on leave from, surprisingly, the British Antarctic Survey, concentrated on the montane habitat, making a census of the birds there which included virtually all previously recorded avifauna from above 5800 feet. He also added fourteen new species to the park's record and found the summit of Mulu a delightful place to work where, with a backcloth of superb views over the lower vegetation, some of the most beautiful endemic species could be closely observed feeding at exotic blooms.

All these studies combine to illustrate how knowledge of density and diversity of birds – which are a comparatively readily identifiable group – can provide a useful index to the overall richness and complexity of different habitats, thus contributing substantially to the management plan.

Other visiting ornithologists concentrated on particular groups of birds.

Few people have ever been lucky enough to see the great argus pheasant, finest of all the pheasants, with its long elegantly patterned tail; but all who came to Mulu must have heard its wild cry ringing out and drowning for an instant all other sounds. The display grounds made by the males were also a familiar sight on the ridges, always a good spot for the men to drop their loads and call for a rest. Geoffrey Davison from the University of Malaya was most anxious to record the rare endemic Bulwer's pheasant (*Lophura bulweri*) whose numbers were thought to be declining so much that it had recently been included in the IUCN *Red Data Book*. In spite of a long and careful search, he never saw or heard one. The nearest he came was when two Berawans who had camped alone on the path up Mulu in the course of ferrying supplies up the mountains, brought him a single tail feather. They had snared and eaten the bird the previous night, but knowing Geoffrey was interested in pheasants had innocently preserved the evidence of their villainy. We constantly reminded the men that they were forbidden to hunt when in our employ, but it is hard to change the habits of a lifetime overnight. Being a patient character Geoffrey did not make a fuss but it must have been a most frustrating moment.

Ben King from the American Museum of Natural History and co-author of *A Field Guide to the Birds of Southeast Asia* wanted to study and collect frogmouths during his brief stay with us. Borneo, with six species, has the greatest diversity of frogmouths anywhere in the world. None had previously been recorded from montane moss forest but Gathorne Medway had reported being woken at Camp Four by something making a penetrating cat-like mew which he failed to see but which might have been a frogmouth. The specially adapted gun which Ben had had sent from America failed to reach us in time, so he took with him Lang, armed with his own somewhat antique single-barrelled twelve-bore shotgun. They spent three nights at Camp Four, mostly in heavy rain, searching by torchlight, whistling an imitation of the frogmouth's call and occasionally receiving an answer, but without getting a glimpse of the bird.

'Once it called from a distance of only four or five metres, but I could not see it in the dense vegetation', Ben wrote to me later:

Since time was short I moved down to Camp Three. There we had rain every night for five nights, mostly precluding searching for night birds. On what we planned as our final night, David Wells, Lang and I started out at 8 pm to see what we could find. Just a hundred metres from camp, I whistled a frogmouth call and got an immediate reply from a bird making the same call that I had heard at Camp Four. But this bird was far more vociferous and came closer. I got tape recordings, but found that the bird responded just as well to our whistle as to the tape. After a while a second bird started calling. The birds would call for a while and come closer and then stop calling and move off. It wasn't until about 1 am that we got a glimpse of a shadow flying from tree to tree. Then an hour or so later we got a clear look at the bird. We asked Lang to collect it for us. He tried but the birds got away. They still kept calling and approaching us and we stayed around until well after dawn in hopes of getting one, but had no luck.

[That night] Lang and I went out at about 8 pm and started whistling again. The bird answered and gradually moved closer and around us. Finally at about 9.30 pm the frogmouth moved on to a perch in the open about fifty metres away and Lang slowly and carefully took aim and fired. The bird dropped immediately. I cleaned it up and wrapped it in cotton.

Next day I skinned the bird and prepared it for preservation. I did not know at that time what it was since the smaller frogmouths are so close in appearance. All I knew was that it didn't quite fit any of the other small frogmouths.

It was only after studying specimens of all the other species of frogmouths at the American Museum of Natural History in New York with Dr Joe Marshall that its uniqueness was apparent. Tally ho! The bird is not yet named or described. It makes seven 'froggies' for Borneo. It's the first new species I've discovered and the first in ten years for Asia.

Truly a most significant ornithological discovery. It was the only bird shot by the expedition.

The most spectacular birds in the park were the hornbills. All eight species are striking birds, fairly easy to identify even by laymen from their size and the distinctive black and white markings of their bodies.

The laboured beating of their wings sounded like swans overhead as they flew over the canopy and several species have a raucous, almost bad-tempered cry which they often emit in flight. Once, however, the Penan walking with me began to imitate a call like pigeons cooing and two white-crested hornbills came and settled nearby. Another time I saw a pair of rhinoceros hornbills fly high over the summit of Api calling to each other, when I was on the ridge at about 5000 feet. This species has an extraordinary casque on its bill coloured bright red and yellow. It is the national bird of Sarawak.

Hornbills are now fully protected but once there was a thriving trade in the casques of the helmeted hornbill (known as the 'mother-in-law' bird because of its hysterical laughing call) which the people of Borneo made into earrings while those exported to China were carved into exquisite ornaments. This trade goes back as far as the T'ang dynasty when hornbill 'ivory' was valued twice as high as elephant ivory.

As well as being good indicators of the health of an ecosystem, birds are also likely in the future to be one of the major attractions for visitors to the park. It was particularly notable that all the species of several of the main groups of Borneo's forest birds were recorded in the park. This was so for the noisy and ubiquitous barbets, the quiet and shy trogons and, of course, the hornbills. In due course, as the primeval forests of South-East Asia are reduced through man's expansion into previously undisturbed regions, the few remaining protected areas such as Mulu will become increasingly valuable, not only as priceless reservoirs for future study but also as a profitable draw for tourists from all over the world and a source of national pride for the government.

11

Reptiles, Fishes and Insects

CROCODILES exist far inland in Borneo. When we first arrived on the Melinau river, the Berawans were sure there were crocodiles in the big pool at Base Camp and were reluctant to swim in deep water. The previous year Sabang's brother had been taken by one near Long Terawan and his mutilated body found some days later. This made us nervous of bathing at first, but we gradually became braver, diving off the raft daily and exploring the underwater caves below the *batu* while the children played on the sandbank opposite. Sightings on the larger river by those passing in boats were fairly frequent, with monsters of twelve up to twenty feet (probably exaggerated) being reported several times. Once or twice people thought they saw crocodiles sliding off the banks of the Melinau itself and swimming under the clear water, but these were probably monitor lizards.

Monitors were a common sight on the rivers, usually glimpsed only for a moment before they dived, but occasionally seen crouched motionless on logs asleep in the sun or hoping to avoid being noticed as a boat passed. One six feet long was caught in a fish trap and examined before being released. A wire netting enclosure was built on the beach and half a dozen keen photographers took up their positions as the end of the trap was opened and we waited for it to step out and pose on the sand. For a moment its head with long forked tongue sticking out was seen; then it ran at high speed straight through the fence and into the river where it disappeared. Only one rather blurred photograph was obtained.

Joan Cramphorn, our fish specialist, had a more dramatic sighting one day when she was alone in camp. A seventeen-foot python, weighing 117 lb, had been found drowned in one of her gill nets in the river on Christmas Eve. Some of the meat was cut up for Christmas dinner instead of the turkey donated by Jacksons of Piccadilly which had failed to arrive in time. It tasted like rather tough chicken but was well received. The skin and remaining meat were left in a large polythene bag on the raft. On Boxing Day everyone except

Joan went down to Long Terawan for a football match – Mulu Members v. Berawans – so that the camp was unusually quiet. On her way to bathe Joan observed two monitor lizards four feet and seven feet long attacking the polythene bag and eating the snakeskin. She was able to watch them for a long time. Even when she disturbed them by a quick movement so that they plunged into the water, they soon came back to continue tearing at the meat and plastic with their sharp teeth. When at last she removed the skin to the laboratory for subsequent examination, the larger lizard swam across the river to the far bank with the polythene bag in its mouth where it vanished into the jungle.

Until the end of the expedition we assumed that these powerful lizards, for all their ferocious, dragonlike appearance, were quite harmless and would never attack man. Then, during our last couple of weeks, a Penan boy was brought to our doctor with severe lacerations on his leg which we were told had been caused by a monitor on which he had trodden while crossing a stream.

The python Joan caught was not the first or the largest we saw. One measuring twenty-two feet was killed on the Tutoh by a group of Penan who gave us some of the meat and the skin, which we would like to have preserved. But it had been so cut up in the killing, which must have been a mighty battle for men armed only with blowpipes and parangs, that we could only measure, photograph and throw it in the river when it began to stink. Other snakes, too, seemed common but none were aggressive and no one was ever bitten. Many were seen swimming across rivers, including an eight-foot hamadryad or king cobra (*Naja hannah*), the world's largest poisonous snake, which Nigel and Mark chased in the jet boat, its distinctive orange throat clearly visible. Pit vipers, which are also fairly poisonous but very sluggish and disinclined to move, often remained motionless in their chosen bush, close to scientists at work, for several days.

One of the rare frightening encounters with snakes happened to Chris Saunders, a veterinary student studying blood parasites in vertebrates. During one hot, sleepy afternoon he walked down the raised pathway behind our longhouse to visit one of the two 'long drop' latrines or *jamban*. As he was preparing to leave again, he suddenly saw a snake suspended in the narrow doorway, effectively cutting off his only escape and apparently ready to strike. He was able to identify it as the dangerous common or Malayan krait (*Bungarus candida*), a specimen of which had been caught near Base Camp a few days before, and which is reputedly even more poisonous than the notorious banded krait (*Bungarus fasciatus*). Evidently it had been lying on the roof, had detected his presence within and had come down to investigate. As Chris backed into the furthest corner of the small square hut, the snake slithered further down towards the floor, then lost its balance and fell through the steps at the entrance to the ground below.

The black and white snakes found in the caves were identified as striped racers (*Elaphe taeniura*). They, like the majority of snakes seen, were back-fanged and therefore much less dangerous. Rat snakes up to eleven feet long, some of which look alarmingly like king cobras, regularly visited Base Camp and sometimes frightened our chickens. One night I went out several times to see what was bothering them before noticing a sizeable snake coiled around their perch watching them as they huddled together at the far end. Convincing ourselves it was a cobra and feeling very brave, Nigel and I caught it with a noose by torchlight and put it in a bag which we hung from the rafters in the kitchen so that it couldn't escape. Kiew Bong Heang, a lecturer in zoology at the University of Malaya, who was studying fishes and frogs with us, returned in the morning, took one look and, pulling it from the bag, said 'quite harmless and very common'. It was released again under the longhouse.

Kiew had interesting ideas about the commercial possibilities of the rain forest. He told me that there was a £10 million world market for frogs' legs, which were seriously over-collected in many places, while efforts to farm frogs had not yet proved very successful. In fact it was his own efforts in that direction which had led him into studying them. Properly culled, frogs could represent a viable crop. Fish, too, he felt were under-exploited in the interior where some excellent large species of carp no longer found in polluted waters could well be farmed, though not, of course, in or near a national park.

The diversity of fish in the rivers and their teeming numbers in the undisturbed upper reaches of the Melinau constantly amazed us. Heading up-river when the water was clear, great shoals could be seen gleaming silver as they darted away from the boat, while sometimes big ones sped ahead of us like porpoises. Most temperate rivers hold no more than a dozen different species of fish, but the rivers in and around the park probably have well over 100. Almost all can be eaten and some were quite delicious. They played a major part in our diet and we ate several which weighed over fifty pounds. The Berawans caught them mainly with nets placed across the mouths of side streams – but not inside the park while working for the expedition – while we tried less successfully with spinners and worms. When the fishing had been poor for a time it was tempting to encourage Joan to use her electric stunning gear and it must be admitted that some of her better catches did go into the pot after due examination.

Julian Dring, who collected frogs assiduously during his two visits, never offered us any of his catch as food. Instead he spent much of the day surrounded by an intrigued audience of Berawans and Penan, injecting his specimens with formalin to preserve them and packing them carefully away. By night the beam of his powerful head-torch could be seen for hour after hour and in all weathers darting from tree to tree as he tracked down his prey, plunging through the undergrowth. For such a gentle, quiet person Julian was an extraordinarily determined and fearless hunter. He also made extensive recordings of frogs' and toads' calls, playing back to us the astonishing mixture of unlikely and often surprisingly loud sounds they made. Between them, he and Kiew identified sixty per cent of known Bornean frogs within the national park.

Turtles are caught and eaten by the longhouse people on the major rivers and sad captives could sometimes be seen in Marudi market. Several species of turtles, tortoises and terrapins are to be found in Mulu, but no one was specifically studying them and few were seen. Only one turtle, probably a Malayan soft-shelled turtle (*Trionyx cartilagineus*), was found in the river at Base Camp when the water level was exceptionally low and we could walk across on the sandy bottom. Inggan caught it near the raft and brought it up to the house, holding it carefully by the rear edge of its shell. It was olive green and about nine inches long, with webbed feet and a proboscis like a short elephant's trunk on the end of its snout, which it kept well back inside its shell. When placed on the ground, the head emerged at the end of an incredibly long neck, as long as the rest of its body, with which it could reach right back almost to its hind legs to deliver quite a powerful bite. We kept it for a time in a glass tank where it buried itself until invisible in the sand at the bottom. Every ten minutes or so the 'trunk' would cautiously poke up followed by the eyes which looked carefully all round. Then very slowly the neck was extended up to the surface until the small nostrils were able to draw a single quick breath, when it retracted rapidly into its shell and became invisible once more.

Much of the zoological research on the expedition was concerned with investigating how the available resources were being shared out within the park. An innate characteristic of tropical rain forest is that, while there are many species present, there are very few individuals of any one species. Competition in nature is largely between members of the same species, as rarely do two kinds of animal try to exploit the forest in exactly the same way.

To study how an animal establishes its own ecological niche, and thus avoids competition, information is needed on where it lives, what are the limits of its resources, in what manner and how often it breeds, and eventually, most significant of all, how many surviving young can it produce in a lifetime and of what does it die.

Ian Swingland from the Animal Ecology Research Group at Oxford, who had been working for the previous four years on the population dynamics of the giant tortoises on Aldabra, chose lizards as the easiest vertebrates to work on in Mulu. At first they seemed a most unpromising choice since they cannot be mist-netted like birds, attracted to lights like moths and other insects or collected by hand like ants and beetles. But with the help of the Penan he developed an original and effective way of catching them. The darts used by the Penan in their blowpipes had a cone of pith shaped to fit exactly inside the pipe. When blown through the pipe this would force the sharp and usually poisoned end of the dart straight towards the prey. By reversing the dart so that the pith travelled in front they found that it still flew true but when striking a small creature like a lizard merely knocked it off the tree and stunned it for a few moments. With their extraordinary skill and accuracy Ian's Penan helpers were able to hit lizards from sixty feet away which, if they had come any closer, would have been disturbed and vanished into the canopy above. This gave him time to examine, identify and sex the lizards before releasing them unharmed when they regained consciousness.

The strangest of the lizards were the flying lizards (*Draco* spp). In these some of the ribs, instead of curving round the body in the usual way, can be extended to support membranes of skin forming so-called wings which they use to glide from tree to tree. Like other gliding creatures of the rain forest such as the flying squirrels, lemurs, frogs and even snakes, this means that they can travel continuously without ever needing to descend to the ground except in some cases to breed. The female flying lizards excavate nests in the soil in which they lay four or five eggs. Their existence also illustrates how enormously long the forests must have remained unchanged for such specialized animals to have evolved.

There are more kinds of butterflies and moths in tropical rain forests than in all the other natural habitats of the world put together. Jeremy Holloway of the Commonwealth Institute of Entomology and author of *Moths of Borneo* spent five months in Mulu. With his light trap and generator he sampled by night at all levels throughout the park, collecting about eighty per cent of the recorded Bornean species of moths, prime target of his survey. Many other insects were also attracted to the light so that the hours he spent by day sorting his night's catch produced interesting and very variable results. Seeing large representative selections of the insects interacting and competing with each other in a small area of forest, all laid out neatly, species by species, in piles on Jeremy's sorting table, revealed yet again the incredible diversity of insects and their intricate relationships with the forest plants. Over twenty species of cicadas, piercers and suckers of sap can be taken in one night in lowland forest, whereas in Britain we have only one; in Jeremy's words 'the crickets and beetles are chewers of foliage, the mantis and the dragon-fly are predators on other insects, and the moths and butterflies have a particular love-hate relationship with the forest in that the adults are vital for pollination, yet the caterpillars eat the leaves and are therefore detrimental to the plants'.

The males of Rajah Brooke's birdwing (*Trogonoptera brookiana*), among the most magnificent of all the butterflies, were quite common at Base Camp. The extreme beauty of their elegant black wings decorated with brilliant green feather-shaped marks crowned by a bright red head contrasted with the squalor of the sludge pit outside the kitchen where they chose to congregate daily to satisfy some special yearnings.

Among my personal favourites were the wood nymphs (*Idea* sp), large floppy grey and white butterflies which drifted from tree to tree like ladies in chiffon dresses, seemingly unaware and unafraid of potential predators. This is because they taste foul, probably through toxins assimilated from their larval plant food. Useful additional projects were always being thought up by some of the departing scientists. One suggestion was that, as butterflies play such an important role carrying pollen between trees as they feed selectively on the same few species, someone should spend a few days following one of these slow-moving nymphs and record each tree on which it settled. I liked the notion of producing a paper entitled 'Pursuing an Idea' but it still remains to be done.

There are several hundred species of butterfly in Borneo and, because so many of them are colourful and fly by day, they are much in evidence. But the moths are numbered in thousands with many species still unrecorded. However taxonomy, the identifying and classifying of moths, was not an end in itself for Jeremy Holloway. This was merely the foundation of the biogeographical and ecological work which interested him more.

At certain times in the recent geological past, especially during the Ice Ages when the sea-level fell markedly, the lands on the Sunda Shelf (Malaya, Sumatra, Java, Borneo) were united as a single land mass; intervening periods of high sea-level split the area into even more islands than now exist. Each time this happened widespread species would be fragmented, each fragment developing along slightly different lines, so when these fragmentary populations were subsequently reunited they co-existed as distinct species.

Species found only at higher altitudes are particularly interesting, the widely separated mountain tops presenting isolated islands of habitat distinct from that of the lowlands. A few moth groups have diversified within these mainly young mountain systems, but the majority have spread from the north, filtering down along the Himalayas and through Burma into Malaysia, or from China via Taiwan and the mountains of the Philippines. A few have spread up from temperate regions of Australia or from the young mountains of New Guinea across central Indonesia where the Oriental and Australasian plant and animal groups meet and intermingle. This Australasian element has far higher representation in the montane floras of Borneo. These biogeographical patterns make Borneo an especially intriguing place to study in many fields.

Henry Barlow, who lives in Kuala Lumpur where he is treasurer of the Malayan Nature Society, collected for a time with Jeremy in Mulu as they had done together before on Mount Kinabalu. He was pleased to catch a moth at 3250 feet which was first discovered in Sumatra in 1920 and had not been seen since until he had collected one eighteen months previously at the same altitude near Kuala Lumpur. His business being the management of several large estates in west Malaysia, he was particularly aware of the importance of understanding moth populations under natural conditions. With the increase in large-scale mono-culture plantations, particularly of oil palm, there are serious risks of major outbreaks of pests and many of these are moths. To date treatment has been by the blanket spraying of chemical pesticides and it has been observed that this practice kills off many more of the moths' predators than the pests themselves. Knowing as much as possible about the natural balance of species may make it feasible to devise systems of cropping which overcome the pest problem by growing a more varied vegetation. The danger is that, even when conserving an area as relatively large as the Mulu National Park, some species which occupy specialized niches are already very rare indeed. Quite small and apparently insignificant changes caused by, for example, the logging and burning of areas some distance away or minor alterations to the micro-climate through clearance, will alter the moth population perceptibly and probably eliminate some species altogether. Sampling of moths therefore can provide yet another rapid method of measuring environmental changes as well as being potentially useful for investigating the ecology of agricultural systems.

Another interesting line of research on lepidoptera was pursued by Alec Panchen from the University of Newcastle-upon-Tyne. As a zoologist with an overriding interest in evolutionary theory he had come to work on butterfly genetics, specializing in the family *Danaidae*. One of the earliest and most studied cases of natural selection ever was that proposed by Bates in 1860. He had noticed for the first time in the Amazon forests that, in addition to species of butterfly which were apparently poisonous, there were unrelated and much rarer species which had evolved to mimic them and thus protect themselves. The danaids on which Alec concentrated possessed a remarkable ability to feed on some highly poisonous plants and store the poisons through to the adult stage when they acted as a deterrent to the bird predators. In addition to the interest of ascertaining how they were able to do this and the theoretical importance from a genetic point of view, the poisons themselves, some of which are very similar to digitalis, might have a use in cardiac medicine. A difficulty arose in preserving the specimens for later analysis back in Newcastle. If they were simply killed in the normal way by slow cooking in the drying oven, the metabolism of the butterfly might de-nature the poisons. The only way was to deep-freeze them rapidly so that the chemicals would not be affected. But we had no deep-freeze at Base Camp. As a result the live butterflies were put in transparent envelopes and taken down-river, ninety miles to Marudi, each time a boat went during Alec's stay. There they were put overnight in Johnny Leong's freezer packed between the ice cubes, to be brought back to camp again with the post next morning. They could then be dried out and stored in silica gel for shipment.

A number of scientists from the British Museum (Natural History) came to study insects and other arthropods. Each revealed an endearing tendency to believe that his or her own speciality was of unique significance. Sometimes they became passionate in the defence of their chosen families. Barry Bolton had a refreshingly individual approach to research work. During the day he spent every waking hour collecting ants on his hands and knees, scrupulously examining every inch of a chosen square yard of soil, bitten from head to foot by mosquitoes, horseflies and leeches, never moving more than a hundred yards from the longhouse. At night, as though reacting to these prolonged periods of immobility and silence, he consumed vast quantities of our precious early supply of beer, while regaling all around with outrageous and hilarious stories followed later still by bawdy songs. Conversation round the table in the evenings was always animated, never acrimonious, but Barry clearly felt that his beloved ants were neglected in favour of more glamorous creatures.

'There are more insect species, over a million, than all other animal species put together' he said.

If bird taxonomy was on the same level as insect taxonomy all the birds would be in one family and it would be a small family. I could show you two ants which are as dissimilar as an elephant and a crocodile and according to vertebrate taxonomic language they are in different classes. Yet all ants are classified in one family.

It's going to take twenty years to work up all I've collected here. Of course they'll be farmed out to people all over the world – I won't do it all myself.

Ants play a very important part in the ecology of all forests, but it's only in rain forests that you have such diversity that they become noticeable. Most people don't have any idea of how many insects there are. I'd like to see visitors to the park take more interest in them. Being small, you have to look for them, but they keep the whole cycle going.

Take any ant and ask what it's good for. From a human aspect it may not be good for anything, but it's a very impressive piece of work and to see it vanish would be a pity. What good are sparrows? What good are people, come to that? Who's made a bigger mess, ants or people?

There were two species of ant which no one could fail to notice. These were, firstly, the unmistakable giant ant (*Camponotus gigas*), common throughout South-East Asia, whose worker 'soldiers', armed with formidable mandibles, can grow to over an inch in length. They travelled everywhere, exploring the kitchen and the *jamban* aggressively, so that new arrivals were often seriously alarmed. In fact they did little damage and seldom hurt anyone, although Gerry Mitton, our first doctor, was bitten on the bottom by one when paying an early visit to the *jamban* and, as she put it, 'nearly had the first aerial view of Mulu'. Much more painful were the fire-ants (*Leptogenys processionalis*), hard to see but with a sting like a wasp. They seemed to come out at night and anyone rash enough to walk outside barefoot or in sandals in the dark was soon likely to start hopping about shouting obscenities.

There are probably more species of ants in Borneo than in the whole North American continent. Those in the latter have been very well collected while no intensive collecting has been undertaken before on the former. Barry found over two hundred species in one hectare around Base Camp and there may be three or four times that number still to be identified throughout the island.

About a quarter of all the world's known animals are beetles and many more await discovery, especially in the tropics. They are a very early group of insect, most of which evolved a hundred million years ago and their roles have not changed much since. Some live as long as fifty years and they are to be found almost everywhere except the sea, living in the vegetation and the soil, deep inside caves and in all fresh waters.

The British Museum (Natural History) is the main institution for naming beetles but collections from Borneo are relatively poor so that naming the material collected on the expedition will be difficult but, once done, useful to the Sarawak Government. They are among the worst pests and can do immense damage to crops, especially when a change is made from shifting agriculture to mono-culture.

Peter Hammond and Jane Marshall came to collect adults and larvae respectively and were well satisfied with what they found. One of Peter's special preoccupations was cowpats which, of course, he knew he would not find in the national park. I fetched him from the airport in a chartered lorry, since the same RAF aircraft carried a load of urgently needed stores. Whenever he saw a cow by the roadside he insisted that we should stop so that, donning a pair of rubber gloves, he could rummage happily in their droppings for half an hour to the intense surprise of our Chinese drivers. 'I can find over fifty beetle species in one cowpat,' he explained 'but it's better if they're not too fresh.'

The larvae Jane collected in the park were even less well-known than the adults and will add greatly to the knowledge of the overall beetle fauna since larvae and adults often do not occur together and relationships can only be laboriously established back in the museum.

Many of the larger beetles we saw were very handsome creatures, which we found irresistible and brought back to Base Camp. Harry Vallack undertook the job of preserving these and other spectacular specimens such as stick insects, preying mantises and crickets when there was no expert with us. The black rhinoceros and other scarabaeid beetles were harmless but huge, with fearsome horns reaching forward like pincers with which they could hook and hold each other in battle. Others, such as the jewel and tortoise beetles had brilliant metallic colours on their shells – green, gold, and red – so that they looked like Fabergé enamelled treasures.

Less striking but equally important were the aphids, bugs and grasshoppers studied by Victor Eastop and Dave Hollis. There were no aphids at all from Sarawak in the British Museum collection and, despite finding numerous species of whiteflies, only twelve aphids were found in the park. They are significant in that more virus diseases of plants are transmitted by aphids than by any other insects. Many are also kept as domestic animals by ants so that there was a direct connection with Barry's work. Aphids and other similar insects which feed on plants excrete surplus sugar as honeydew. This is the Biblical manna which is still collected in the Middle East and used in confectionery. When stored it is possible that it may become contaminated with ergot which used to be used as a type of hallucinogen. Victor had a nice theory that the trespasses for which forgiveness is asked in the Lord's Prayer referred to people who rather fancied eating stored manna contrary to the specific instructions given in Exodus.

I found snippets of information like that, revealed by the scientists as they went about their routine and often apparently monotonous tasks, one of the best things about being on the expedition. Their wide experience and funds of stories never allowed our daily lives to seem dull, while their acute powers of observation meant that we all became much more aware of our surroundings. Dave's main interest was sap-feeding bugs (*Sternorhyncha*), especially jumping plant lice (psyllids), primitive little creatures which are extremely host-specific. This means that each psyllid species is capable of living only on one species of plant, so that with the tremendous botanical diversity of the rain forest they have quite a problem finding another host plant in order to feed and breed.

A useful spin-off of this specialization was that Dave could make suggestions to botanists about plant taxonomy based on his insect taxonomy, since if he found two similar species feeding on two different species of plants then he could question the botanical judgement on which the classification had been based. He was also one of the first to notice the speed with which even our relatively non-destructive presence was affecting the balance of nature. A bare three months after we had cleared it, he found several species of grasshoppers on the helipad which had been introduced from some distance outside the park, probably riding up on longboats from Long Terawan. Jeremy Holloway found the same thing moth-trapping in areas which had been recently cleared, as did Barry Bolton with 'tramp' species of ants and Fred Wanless, also from the British Museum (Natural History), with his spiders.

Most people are scared of spiders and it was refreshing to have an expert who could reassure us that he had not found a dangerous one yet and who handled them as gently and affectionately as the rest of us treated kittens or small birds. The notorious black widow was apparently absent from the park and Fred said reassuringly that it would have turned up under the longhouse if it had been anywhere. Bird-eating spiders and other large hairy ones were rarely seen, although Shane did find what she was convinced was a tarantula in her bed and most of the long-stay members had a resident giant orbweb spider in their rooms with idiosyncratic habits. Mine used to swing its web violently back and forth when disturbed, like a monkey shaking the bars of its cage; Nigel swore his spat loudly at him during the night; while the one in the Proctor family's *bilek* wove an elegant canopy over Katy's cot.

Our most eccentric invertebrate pet was Belinda, a giant forest scorpion (*Heterometrus longinanus*), five inches long and the third largest in the world, which ambled across the floor one day at lunchtime. While the rest of those present took ignominiously to the table Jo Anderson and I chased her back and forth under a *kajang* wall until we were able to secure her in a large transparent box. There she promptly gave birth to twenty-six live white babies which she fed on a milky fluid secreted from near her mouth – the first recorded birth in captivity of this species. Nursed with great skill by Jo, who would fearlessly pick Belinda up by the sting when tidying their home, eighteen of the young survived the many hazards of a scorpion's childhood, not least among which is the fact that when the 'milk' dries up after about two weeks their mother tries to eat them. Packing them carefully and separately among his underclothes and socks, Jo brought them safely back to Exeter University where they are still doing well. On his return to Mulu for a second visit, Jo was lucky enough to collect an even larger – six inch – male scorpion of the same species. But during the night which he spent with friends of the expedition at Brunei on his way home it escaped and in spite of an exhaustive search through the flat was not found again in time for his flight. Our friends were not comforted by Jo's assurances that it would clear out any cockroaches and one of our useful overnight stops was lost to us!

Although we had so many specialists with us, the invertebrate fauna of Mulu must still be considered poorly known. Even in areas which are well studied their conservation is still in its early stages and Mulu is a splendid place for further detailed studies. Add to this the enormous botanical, geomorphological and other zoological interest of the place and we can only feel deeply privileged to have been allowed to work in such a fascinating environment.

Of all the 115 scientists who took part I have only been able to mention briefly the work of a few. The expedition was planned for them and the way they responded in terms of enthusiasm and volume of work done was more than admirable. What I had not fully expected was the pleasure we all derived from associating with such stimulating company and the many lifelong friendships which developed.

12

Tourism, Park Management and the Penan

ALL were agreed that the park must be saved and protected for the future. Opinions differed as to the best way of ensuring this. Rather like politicians, our scientists' views ranged from the arch-conservative protectionist approach of wishing to keep everyone out of the park, except for occasional qualified people, to radical talk of cable cars over the mountains and through the caves carrying quantities of tourists. It was the key question which exercised all our minds and good that it should be debated long and ardently in the field. Our prime belief and *raison d'être* in Sarawak was to prepare a draft management plan for the park and, while a clearly necessary prerequisite of this was to gather as much information as possible in the time available about its structure and composition, at the end of the day we still had to recommend how it should best be managed so that the maximum benefit is gained by all who wish to use it.

With many organisms minor disturbances were not of great moment. As long as the trees were not cut down, pollutants introduced or the climate subtly changed by alterations to the countryside around the park, they would survive. Lichens and frogs, orchids and butterflies would continue to thrive even if quite large numbers of people came to look at them, provided of course they were not allowed to collect or damage them. With others, such as the larger mammals, the presence of increasing numbers of people could mean that they became even wilder and harder to see than they are at present, although paradoxically some species, especially monkeys, can become much tamer if the introduction of tourism is accompanied by a ban on hunting. The greatest danger in bringing many visitors into the park is certainly the lasting damage they themselves may do to the physical environment. Trails degenerate rapidly under the pressure of feet, causing erosion and water runnels. Improving paths with raised walkways, steps and ladders is not only expensive and often ugly but unless materials are introduced from outside the very process itself degrades the immediate surroundings of the path – the forest the visitors see – by removing much of the timber. An even more disastrous impact could be made by thoughtless damage done in the caves, where fragile stalactites may be broken off, delicate calcite formations trodden on and the results of millenia of natural processes destroyed in a moment.

Apart from a few spectacular views, the wonders of the caves and the joy of travelling on an undisturbed river, there is not a great deal in Mulu to attract the average tourist. The magic of the rain forest is not immediately apparent; a trained eye is often needed to observe the mysteries behind the overpowering quantities of wet green vegetation; and there are many much more accessible parks and gardens close to the coasts and cities in Malaysia and South-East Asia. Nonetheless as time goes by the value of the timber in the park will increase dramatically and envious eyes will focus on it. It will be argued that potential wealth is being locked away for no good reason and should instead be exploited. While the scientific argument – that the conservation of wilderness areas and gene pools and the huge benefit to all that may accrue from studies undertaken in such places as Mulu far outweigh the short-term gain – may be valid, the support and interest of ordinary members of the public who have seen and enjoyed the place could carry even more weight. In any case people are going to want to go there and proper arrangements must be made for their convenience, control and enlightenment.

The initial responsibility for preparing the draft management plan lay with Robb Anderson. This document, consisting of texts, maps and photographs with appendices of checklists of the more important groups of plants and animals was submitted to the World Wildlife Fund (who funded it) in July 1979. It is a strategy which spells out in a programmed way what land management and patrols should be carried out by forest guards and other staff of the Forest Department in order to maintain the unique habitats found there. Particularly sensitive or rich areas are delimited and it is hoped that these will be protected absolutely. Where visits of Malaysian and overseas tourists are permitted close monitoring will study their impact. Some effects, such as the pressure on trails, can be foreseen and is spelled out in the management plan with proposals as to what should be done to counterbalance the damage.

All of this management costs money and the Sarawak Government is aware of this, but the amount annually expended is small compared to the richness of the natural beauty that this state is lucky enough to possess. Tourists can be controlled. So too can the shifting cultivators that will no doubt try to penetrate from the Limbang valley, but strong measures will be needed if the damage visible over so much of Borneo, especially in Kalimantan, is to be avoided.

As the draft management plan points out, the park is already used by a large number of indigenous people, some of whom go there to hunt and gather produce while others actually live within its boundaries. All have rights and privileges granted under the Park Charter. This aspect of the park's present and future worried all who went there, especially in so far as it related to the still nomadic groups of Penan.

An irreconcilable problem arises concerning the Penan and their future use of the park. They are in many ways superb conservationists, better able than anyone to judge the fine balance between their needs from available wild food resources and a cropping rate which would prevent regeneration. Without this knowledge and the other controls which have kept their population stable, they would long ago have hunted the wild life to extinction and destroyed the stands of sago upon which they depend for carbohydrate. However two things are now happening which are not compatible with the satisfactory future running of a major national park. Already some Penan have acquired shotguns which are probably more effective than blowpipes for hunting and certainly cause more disturbance. As a result, game in the lowlands and more accessible parts of the park is becoming scarce and very shy. At the same time the deforestation of surrounding areas is forcing more Penan to move into the park in search of the remaining relatively undisturbed forests. Their increasing presence undoubtedly diminishes the value of the park to the zoologist interested in observing larger mammals in the wild.

Fortunately a highly qualified team from the Sarawak Museum joined us before the end of the expedition to make a survey of the Penan and to determine the effects of their presence in the park. They were led by Peter Kedit, the government ethnologist, under whom ethnographical, ethnobotanical and human ecological studies were carried out among most of the nomadic and settled Penan using the park. In addition Doctor Alec (A.J.U.) Anderson of the Sarawak Medical Service undertook a nutritional survey of the same communities. Their excellent subsequent reports produced a wealth of interesting and thought-provoking material concerning the sensitive and difficult subject of the Penans' future.

As with most of our other baseline studies the first essential was to establish the numbers involved. Before going to Mulu we had tried to find out how many Penan there were likely to be in the area. Information from those scientists who had collected there in the past indicated that we might not meet more than an occasional nomadic group numbering only some twenty or thirty in all. Tom Harrisson, before his untimely death in 1976, had even stated in a letter to John Hemming that all Sarawak nomads were already settled. For the first couple of months after we arrived and set up Base Camp we, too, saw no Penan, except for the settled families at Long Iman. But the Berawans told us that there were groups of nomads around and we saw the remains of their abandoned *sulap* or temporary shelters in several places, including the site of our own longhouse on the Melinau river. It was only after Nyapun first quietly entered camp on 17 August 1977, seeking work, that we began to realize how many Penan there actually were. His own immediate family gave us the first clue, when he revealed that he had ten living brothers and sisters, all with children. His elderly parents, who were at that time still alive, although his father died during the year, had forty-six grandchildren, so that known numbers of their offspring with their husbands, wives and children numbered seventy-one. There were then the families of the respective spouses to be accounted for as well as the other groups of whom we began to hear news and occasionally meet on the further boundaries of the park, up the Tutoh river, around Long Seridan and on the Medalam.

Estimates of Penan numbers began to grow alarmingly, with figures of 600 in the immediate vicinity of the park and up to 2000 in the whole of the Baram region being suggested. With the probability of a rapidly expanding population from improved access to medical services and more Penan moving towards Mulu under pressure from logging operations, the future for both the people and the wild life looked grim. It seemed that only a rapid settlement and retraining programme, with all the inevitable disruption of their society and resultant social problems, would save the day.

However the Sarawak Government teams' surveys began to put things in a healthier perspective. Many of the Penan only use the park intermittently for hunting and gathering produce; some, living closer, spent up to half their time inside it, while only a few live there all or most of the time. By dividing the Penan into 'full time', 'partial' and 'occasional' users they arrived at a figure of not more than 140 Penan or about twenty families who might be in the park at any given time. This gives a ratio of one Penan to every 1.5 square miles of territory which, as Peter Kedit says in his report 'cannot indeed be considered to be too restricting for the Penan, nor would it cause undue imbalance of the Park's ecosystem'.

Nonetheless the problems of their impact on the fauna and flora and of their own future remain, and certain decisions need to be taken urgently. There is no evidence of any serious impact on the smaller mammals of the park by man. The larger mammals on the other hand are hunted energetically by the Penan and by Berawans entering from the south, by Muruts and increasing numbers of Iban from the north and to a much lesser extent by Kelabits from the east. All the latter peoples use shotguns exclusively while, with only a few exceptions, the Penan use blowpipes. Alec Anderson suggests that wild life is probably in far more danger from shotgun users than from the Penan and that 'it may well be proper to ban the use of firearms completely in the Park'. Yet David Labang produced figures based on observations of the amount of game killed by two Penan families during a ten-day sample period which indicated startlingly high results. But he was extrapolating from a much larger assessment of Penan numbers in the park and the later Sarawak Museum survey figures painted a far less gloomy picture. The main emphasis in all hunting is on pig which, while seasonal as they migrate to some extent in search of fruit, appear not to be greatly threatened. Monkeys, however, also play a large part in the Penan diet. They are now protected within the park so that the Penan when they hunt them do so illegally, even though they may not know it. Even if no action is taken on this by the authorities for the time being, the day must come when a replacement source of protein is found for the Penan as hunting activities are reduced and certain species barred to them.

The chief food of all the Penan is the starch from palm stems prepared mainly from the common wild sago (*Eugeissona utilis*) and supplemented with various other rarer species. Even the settled Penan at Long Iman, who have been cultivating hill paddy rice for some ten years, collect sago from far away in order to supplement their poor rice crop. For rice is a difficult crop for beginners and the Penan do not share the overwhelming predeliction for it shown by nearly all other Sarawak and Malay peoples. The scope for teaching them to grow other crops such as maize, tapioca, bananas, beans, sweet potatoes and pumpkins is enormous and opens up an interesting and potentially valuable agricultural future. They have a wide knowledge of edible and medicinal plants, as was shown by the Sarawak Museum team's ethnobotanical studies, and it might be possible to bring some of these into cultivation before the information is lost or forgotten. Above all there are still large stands of sago growing wild and these could rapidly be supplemented by planting local and introduced varieties on land allocated to the Penan near the park. The Long Iman Penan are already trying to do this but only in a very small way.

Both the Government reports on the Penan spoke of the urgent need for land to be set aside for those Penan who wished to settle and pointed out how valuable these areas would be as buffer zones to protect the park. Many of the Penan are interested in the idea of giving up their nomadic way of life and becoming settled farmers and they are conscious of considerable pressure from many of those with whom they come in contact to do so. But they are also very well aware of the difficulties and dangers involved, realizing that without proper medical, educational and agricultural facilities they may well end up worse off. Whatever the Government decides it seems clear that change should be introduced as slowly and as sympathetically as possible so that transitional phases and the adoption of a new lifestyle may be accompanied by the provision of proper assistance.

The area which has been made into the Gunung Mulu National Park comprises a large part of the traditional hunting ground of the Penan. In many conversations they stated fervently that it was their land and that without it they would starve. If this happened they would become a burden upon the Government, adding further to the great number of malnourished shifting agriculturalists in the country. The first priority, therefore, would seem to be to establish their rights to land and to continue hunting, albeit with certain restrictions to accord with the game and national park laws. Change is coming inevitably to them. The park exists and will continue to be used, bringing visitors who will influence them in the process of bringing employment. A road is planned to run through the park joining the Baram to the Limbang and this will expose them still further to modernization as well as increasing vastly the dangers of shifting cultivators moving in and complicating the management of the park. In time their cultural heritage, their gentle, retiring characters and their ability to live in total harmony with their environment will be affected. It was good to see these qualities defended so eloquently in Peter's report where he stated 'if they are lost due to rapid cultural change and the complete disorientation of the Penan people, it will be not only a loss to Malaysia but also to Mankind'.

The problems arising from the fundamental transition of a people to a different way of life, especially where it has concerned the settlement of a previously nomadic society, have seldom if ever been satisfactorily resolved anywhere in the world. The enlightened approach of the Sarawak Government, as revealed in Peter and Alec's reports, leads me to hope that the Penan may be an exception. The solutions they propose to the difficulties make it seem that they are not insuperable. While asserting the absolute right of those Penan who do not wish to settle to continue a nomadic way of life, they point out that their numbers are relatively small and may well not exceed what the park can sustain without serious damage to the wild life. Moreover if hunting by the other neighbouring peoples is reduced and buffer zones for the exclusive use of the Penan established around the park, their territory would be secured. Further, to the east of the park, there is a sizeable area of wild and unoccupied country before the Kelabit Highlands are reached which, with certain other empty territories, could be set aside for their use.

It is those who choose to take the first steps on the road to becoming settled who need the most help and understanding. Everyone hopes that the development of the park will bring economic benefits to the region from the employment of local people by the Forest Department and as guides as well as through the provision of river transport and accommodation. Although the Berawan and other longhouse communities are ready and well able to take advantage of these opportunities, the incomparable knowledge and skills of the Penan should not be neglected. No one knows the park better than they do nor is better qualified to assess what hunting may be taking place and what effects visitors are having on the fauna. They worked willingly and tirelessly for the expedition and, though some members preferred to have Berawans with them in view of their knowledge of English and cheerful companionship, properly trained and supervised Penan could form the nucleus of an expert corps of park wardens. This would begin to compensate them for the loss of meat denied them through certain species being protected.

There are many societies in the Far East, notably in New Guinea and Sumatra, whose economies depend on sago and pig. Often both are farmed. Usually the sago is swamp sago (*Metroxylon sagu*), which can be grown far inland and is in fact sometimes purchased by the Long Iman Penan from Berawans at Long Terawan. It seems likely that the Penan could grow this satisfactorily as well as the more familiar hill sago. Introducing the concept of domesticated pigs might be harder, but if successful this could be the fastest way of reducing pressure on the wild life. Fishing is a relatively new activity for the Penan, although the settled community at Long Iman are now quite successful at it and fish play an increasing role in their diet. As we found, the upper reaches of the rivers are exceedingly rich in fish. These should be stringently protected against the illegal use of *tuba* (derris) poisoning, as has regrettably already happened on the Limbang side of the park and no fishing at all should be allowed inside the park itself, so that at least in the headwaters breeding stocks of most species may survive.

An outlet for the many beautiful artifacts they make would be another source of revenue. The finest baskets, mats and blowpipes in Borneo are traditionally made by the Penan, but all too often they are woefully exploited when they try to sell them, being paid derisory sums or forced to exchange them for a little salt or rice. We established a set of prices based on those which could be obtained after a fair haggle in Marudi. Members of the expedition and visitors to Base Camp were asked to pay no more or less than these, a system which the Penan welcomed and never tried to abuse. Up until 1966 there used to be an annual government-organized and price-controlled market, or *tamu* at the mouth of the Melinau to which Penan came from far and wide to trade at fair prices. Many of them expressed the wish that the *tamu* should be brought back. There seems to be an insatiable demand for good-quality Penan goods on the coast and this is likely to increase with the growth of tourism. But it is important that a fair agency is used to pay proper prices and see that the quality of workmanship is maintained if the market is not to degenerate.

Weaving baskets and mats consumes large quantities of rattans which again will need protection, at least within the park. A solution might be to encourage and help the Penan to cultivate rattans on land outside the park as is done already in peninsular Malaysia and the Philippines.

A most important point made in both reports is that educational plans for both Penan adults and children should take their special needs into account. Experience elsewhere, for example in the USA with Amerindians, has shown that children from a radically different culture, however bright they may be, suffer academically when introduced to schools dominated by others. Schooling is also a danger since too much enforced absence from his parents means that a child fails to learn the traditional skills necessary for survival in the forest. If his schooling is then unsuccessful he will end up with the worst of both worlds. No one who met the attractive and intelligent Penan children who invaded our camp from time to time, cheerfully interested in everything that was going on, but always behaving with impeccable manners, could doubt that special dedicated teachers in a special school on the spot would be able to release much hidden talent.

For the parents too there are things it will be necessary to learn. Apart from the whole range of possible agricultural futures, the transition from a nomadic to a settled life involves an entirely new approach to hygiene. During the measles epidemic we saw and smelt the appalling effect of groups remaining in the same place for more than a few weeks. If clothes are to be worn in order to conform, then they will need to be washed and soap will have to be bought. For trade and understanding of money, basic arithmetic and perhaps some reading and writing will be necessary.

It is in the area of health and medicine that all the Penan, whether settled or still nomadic, most need and seek help. Increased contact with the surrounding population and indeed, if tourism is to develop, with people from all over the world, will introduce a whole spectrum of new health risks and diseases. Changing diets and lifestyles will bring deficiencies and stresses with which their existing remedies will not be able to cope. If their nutritional level is to improve – and it is by no means certain that it will, at least in the short term – then the Penan population could begin to increase rapidly imposing further stresses, unless contraception is provided. Already this is a subject of great concern to Penan and Berawan women alike, which they regularly discussed with our expedition doctors. The Sarawak Medical Service Report cites one nomadic Penan wife who spent nearly three weeks walking most of the way to Limbang and back in order to obtain a supply of the Pill and was charged a substantial sum on arrival. The report recommends that all contraceptive tablets should be supplied free of charge to all in remote rural areas. In the case of the Penan the need is especially great, since they have a tendency to produce relatively large infants and without skilled care many mothers die.

Iodized salt is another urgent need since Alec found very high goitre rates among the Penan and this is the only effective solution. One encouraging finding was that malaria was almost non-existent and this is due to the excellent work of the Malaria Control staff who visited us twice during the expedition, impressing us with their conscientious approach under very difficult conditions.

In sum, the Penan problem, though fraught with moral, social and practical difficulties, is far from insoluble. The main need is a realistic and sensitive approach. Both reports conclude that the Penan, who are at the receiving end of pressures which they neither created nor fully understand, deserve special consideration and attention from a specifically instituted authority created to look after their affairs and protect their legal rights.

13

Looking Back

LOOKING back over the months spent in Mulu generates a lifetime of memories. For a while it was our whole life, bounded by the rivers and the mountains, when we forgot families, friends and jobs at home. Fifteen months is a long time for an expedition to run nowadays, when rapid communications and the speed of life make us less well equipped to tolerate change and isolation. One hundred and forty members coming and going, plus as many local employees and a steady stream of visitors, is a lot of people to cope with. With ages ranging from two to seventy, and often with a 50:50 ratio between the sexes at Base Camp, it might all have been a recipe for disaster. Instead our confined world was a happy one where personalities developed and unexpected talents were revealed. Shy, retiring academics lost their inhibitions and blossomed of a Saturday night to sing long-forgotten songs or organize elaborate games with sticks and bottles. Members of a dozen different nationalities pitched in to produce exotic dishes in the kitchen. The blend of races and characters, contrasting with the solitude of weeks of lonely field work, broke down barriers between people with quite disparate interests and views of the world.

The satisfaction of our encapsulated lives was such that many regretted the need to readjust to their normal existence. After living for so long in shabby comfortable clothes thrown on in a few seconds in the early dawn, shaving off beards, wearing a suit and tie and travelling to work seemed a greater effort than before. All expressed a desire to return one day and felt a continuing commitment to Mulu.

We lived in a teeming world of science, where the things that mattered to us were urgent and compelling, effective research into the astonishing and beautiful ways of nature in its ultimate diversity. Problems were immediate and, once resolved, forgotten. We worked, all of us, harder than we had before imagined possible: the scientists, seized by the pressing need to cram as much into their limited time as available facilities allowed; those in support wrestling twenty-four hours a day with logistical requirements, stretching our limited resources of labour, transport, food and fuel in a ceaseless effort to satisfy the scientists' needs.

Our links with the outside world were the radio, helicopter flights and the river. The first two were heavily dependent on atmospherics, the weather, breakdowns and demands with a higher priority. Only the river led surely to the coast, twisting and turning back upon itself as though seeking any alternative outlet, but providing our one sure escape.

The river is changing and so are the people who live along it. The interior is being simultaneously opened up and denuded. Roads are being pushed inland and along the coast so as to link one end of Sarawak with the other. Transport on the rivers becomes faster and reaches more isolated communities. Logging camps spring up further and further inland, sending out a tangled network of bulldozed tracks along the ridges to extract the trees.

At the same time the cost of living far up-river increases as fuel prices rise, while the chance of well-paid jobs in the oilfields and coastal towns encourages young people to move down-river. Agriculture, already being affected by the widespread loss of forests, the traditional source of new land for clearance, is further hit by the loss of manpower.

On the Tutoh and its tributary the Apo, longhouses and lumber camps already alternate. Almost all the land is allocated in concessions for logging and its character is changing fast. Already, on a still day, the sound of bulldozers could sometimes be heard from the higher ridges of Mulu and Api. The qualities and traditional hospitality of the longhouse people endure, in spite of all the modernizing pressures, so that travellers can always be sure of a welcome. Wherever we stopped, due to breakdowns, rainstorms or nightfall, we were always fed and accommodated. The only price was the expectation that we would take part in an impromptu party and talk far into the night about the world outside, the new national park and the changes which we, coming from the one to study the other, could see approaching.

Long Terawan was both our closest and most regular port of call. We often stayed there on our way up-river or went down at weekends when one of our Berawan friends was being married or for the naming ceremonies which were from time to time arranged to honour us. The names we were given, to the accompaniment of songs, speeches, feasts and much *borak* drinking, were those of legendary folk-heroes – warriors and maidens from the dim past, whose heroic exploits in the pursuit of head-hunting and love affairs have been handed down in myth and song. Nigel and I were Tebengang and Oyau Abeng respectively, the loyal squire and his immortal brother the Prince of the Mountain who could grow a new limb if one was cut off in battle. John and Sue were Senan, our elder brother and Aping his inamorata. Gerry, the much respected lady doctor, was Bungan, an unattainable beauty who lived in a cave on Api, guarded by magic spells.

The reason the Berawans gave us new names, they said, was so that they would remember us. Our own names were either difficult to recall or similar to the common Christian names now used by many of them in addition to their ancient family ones.

The interior of Borneo is described in the *Encyclopaedia Britannica* as 'one of the least known parts of the world' and 'one of the hardest countries in the world to move around in on foot'. Skimming along in the jet boat, as the sunset illuminated the approaching mountains, Mulu seemed like a fairyland where all things were possible, where demi-gods had wrestled with giants and flown from peak to peak. In camp, surrounded by experts, we sometimes felt that it was all an open book, that understanding what was there and how it all fitted together was simply a matter of recording, analysing and assembling facts. And yet the rain forest is a mysterious place and no one will ever know it all. The breadth of scientific knowledge needed is beyond the capacity of one man, one group or even one nation. Those of us who came from the well-ordered countryside of temperate climates often found the teeming life of the forests subduing and alien so that, even when we could rationalize the sounds and feelings we experienced, the fear of the unknown still remained.

Those who lived and hunted there had a deeper, more intimate knowledge of the forest, and for the Penan it was home. I remember the shock I felt when cutting a new trail to Hidden Valley one day with two Berawans and thinking ourselves to be in a piece of forest not previously visited by man, we came out to a shallow river. There, playing unconcernedly in the water, dabbling under stones for shrimps, were Anyi, Nyapun's pretty little six-year-old daughter, and her baby sister. They looked as self-assured and tranquil as they had some days before at Base Camp, or as any children would playing in a suburban sandpit. All our combined academic wisdom, our modern equipment and safety rules suddenly seemed absurd and artificial beside such serenity and harmony. But even this idyllic scene does not give a true picture of life in the rain forest. The Penan have fears and anxieties too about the present and the future. Danger lurks, accidents happen and change is coming.

We were lucky that there were no serious accidents. Sometimes disaster was not far away. Falls on the steep limestone only resulted in cuts and scratches but could easily have been fatal or caused broken bones. During the February floods several boats capsized and their heavily-booted occupants were swept away to be rescued clinging to the bank downstream. Even bathing from the raft held hidden dangers as David Labang proved one day when, in a few minutes, he caught a poisonous snake (a krait) and a sizeable scorpion in the shallows where we all paddled and washed.

The presence of our doctors with their rules for hygiene and regular inspections meant that upset stomachs and infections were kept to a minimum, though Dengue fever, when it struck, laid several Europeans low and a few had to be flown out to hospital by helicopter. Perhaps the most dangerous disease encountered was *Histoplasmosis*, an infection of the lungs contracted in caves, which made Marjorie Sweeting very ill and was not diagnosed until her return to England. The threat of this should be borne in mind by future visitors to the caves.

The doctors were always conscious that the help they were able to give the Berawans and the Penan would cease with the expedition and that they should not create a dependency on medical services not yet available so far up-river. The Penans' resilience when they developed high fevers was impressive and they recovered in a day or two, but conversely they could become very ill with our common cold to which they seemed to have little resistance and the measles epidemic hit them hard. Parasitic worms were common among them and impossible to eradicate due to immediate re-infection, although several attempts were made. One of the more unlikely regular sights at Base Camp was a whole family of Penan reporting to the doctor's surgery, each bearing a carefully-labelled jar containing a stool sample.

Diversity was the spice of Mulu life and the trees gave it the necessary stability. Without them there would be little there of note save for the rocks and caves. Under their canopy swarmed the prolific assemblage of plants and creatures protected by the law from extinction. We set out to learn as much as we could about this unique virgin area, believing it to have a value out of all proportion to its size, and in the process falling under the spell of its beauty and fascination. An expedition is itself a living thing, having a finite life and an identity all its own. Our experiences in Mulu, the friendships formed, the exciting discoveries, the beauty perceived and the sheer fun we had have forged links between a wide assortment of people which will not easily be broken by time and distance. Our united hope is that we may have helped, while adding to the sum of human knowledge, to secure the future of a rich and wonderful place.

Bridging the various culture gaps was not as difficult as some had expected. Our peculiar interests and odd obsessions with earth and water, grubs and leaves, were soon accepted, while we quickly learnt to tolerate the fascinated stares we attracted and the constant lack of privacy. At times our gross ill manners, either through ignorance or irritation, must have grated on people throughout Sarawak for whom courtesy was second nature, but we were never made to feel unwelcome. Indeed accepting the lavish hospitality we were universally offered was often a trial in itself, particularly in my own case where, with the Berawans, it so often involved the consumption of excessive quantities of *borak*. While our members often found the food in sub-camps rather Spartan the Berawans found it strange that we could do without rice at least twice a day, for which they had an almost infinite capacity. In longhouses and Penan camps we ate strange and unfamiliar foods, snake and monkey, squirrels, rats and very ancient pieces of pork gristle, only sometimes baulking at the choicer morsels, while our companions for their part politely omitted to comment on the tastelessness of our own tinned meats.

Our mutual dependence was heavily one-sided. For all our scientific knowledge, most of us would have been helpless and lost on our own in the forest, spending all our time simply surviving with no opportunity for research work. Instead we were spoiled by our attentive helpers, expecting tea within minutes of making camp, food cooking on a fire skilfully made from wet wood, our beds set up with a table and candle for writing up notes and leaks in the roof or camp sheet dutifully plugged at all hours of the night. Only a few of our members were equally at home in a flowering as opposed to a concrete jungle. Robb Anderson was one of these, having travelled the length and breadth of Sarawak during his years in the Forest Service. As the man who had first recognized the scientific potential of Mulu, fought for its establishment as a national park and suggested it as the site for our expedition, he was pleased to see so much being done. But women and children were not part of his concept of life in the forest and he avoided Base Camp as much as possible during his visits. On one notable occasion he, descending the mountain alone, passed Lady Hawley, the British High Commissioner's wife, on her way up. Politely raising his battered hat with a terse 'Good-day', he hurried on down. When he arrived back I asked if he had met anyone. He muttered, 'Saw some woman,' as though admitting to having passed an un-exploded bomb.

The Hawleys were among the distinguished visitors we received who flew in from time to time by helicopter to see what we were up to. Others included Joseph Yong, the Director of Forests, Michael Pocock, the Chairman of Shell Transport and Trading, and John Hunt, President of the Royal Geographical Society. These visitations were usually an excuse for those present to take the day off and accompany our guests to the Deer Cave, followed by a picnic on the delightful stream which crosses the path halfway. One of the most memorable was that of our patron, Edward Shackleton, returning forty-six years later to the scene of his remarkable first ascent of Mulu in 1932. Six of his Berawan companions were still there and able to meet him briefly at Long Terawan, though sadly the jet boat let us down and we failed to reach the party they had arranged in his honour when the still remembered *pantun* or epic song telling of his feat was to be sung. For all the great events which had intervened since his first visit, the Second World War, the Japanese occupation, the burning and rebuilding of their longhouse, the huge expansion of the oil industry on the coast, their lives had not changed radically from those days and the memory of them was still fresh. Now the pace of change is accelerating. The new road will pass close to Long Terawan before it crosses the park. Already it has reached the Tinjar river less than thirty miles away and during our last few months we received several visits from Japanese contractors surveying its proposed route onwards. With trucks and buses roaring past daily instead of a boat every few weeks, with electricity, telephones and television the past may fade more quickly, swamped in the urgency of the present. Perhaps this time we who came and went will remember it all more clearly than those who stayed. Maybe we will have helped them to come to terms with the future.

Ten years previously to ours, another major expedition had been organized by the Royal Geographical Society and the Royal Society to examine a section of the Mato Grosso in Brazil. When they left, the forest they had worked in was cut down and burned and the land cleared for cattle farming. In spite of the scientists' urgent pleas to preserve even their study area and camp as a research station, everything was destroyed. The features they had named, the streams and paths, disappeared; the information they had gathered and their warnings about the dangerous effects of deforestation were totally ignored by the settlers who moved in as soon as the expedition left, to 'develop' the land in their own way. Their forebodings have been well borne out during the last decade as Brazil has continued to waste the vast asset of her forests and only now, when it may be too late, are some wiser counsels beginning to prevail.

We were infinitely more fortunate in this as in so many other respects. Mulu is a national park and will remain so. The Sarawak Government is interested in building on what we began together, in saving at least some of the virgin forests from destruction and in promoting further research into the treasury stored there. While the momentum of environmental destruction world-wide cannot be halted overnight and irreplaceable species will continue to be lost at an alarming rate, such an enlightened approach allows for hope that attitudes may be changing.

Our Base Camp, too, was demolished at the end as had always been agreed. It was on land outside the national park which did not belong to the Forest Department. Most of the materials used were untreated with preservative and only designed to last a year, so that the supports and timbers were already invaded by termites and beginning to shake. Our temporary hygienic arrangements were stretched so that there was a danger of disease building up. Had a group of Penan settled there, as some indicated a wish to do, extreme squalor would have been a likely outcome. Berawan or other settlers moving to a site so near the park would have undermined the concept of buffer zones and encouraged further hunting. And so, sadly, we destroyed all we had built on the banks of the Melinau. Dismantling the longhouse around the last departing scientists, we crated up specimens and valuable equipment which had to be shipped home. Re-usable materials were stored across the river next to the Forest rest-house, our laboratory. Some were used by Inggan to construct a house for himself as the first official park warden, while plans were being drawn up for a proper long term park headquarters. All the endless nails which had been hammered in were pulled out, planks and roofing sheets neatly piled up, water tanks and piping dismantled and rubbish pits filled in. The walkways were taken down and with all the other old timbers, *atap* and *kajang* partitions, heaped on bonfires and burned. The site of the garden was cleared; only the papaya tree Marika had brought from Brunei, which had produced a fine crop of fruit, was left standing incongruously in the open. All our accumulated possessions were either given away or sold and all man-made litter on the ground carefully gathered up and added to the fire. By the end there was only a small clearing, less than half the size of the helipad opposite. It had been mature forest before we came. If left undisturbed it would soon revert to forest again, indistinguishable from that around it to all but expert eyes.

Having all pulled out in a fleet of longboats a week earlier, Nigel, Shane, Philip and I flew back for a final check. It was a clear day and we were able to go high up the mountain to Camp Four. While the RMAF helicopter perched on the narrow ridge, its rotor still turning, we ran down to the empty hut to collect a last British Museum packing case. The camp was clean and tidy but eerie in its abandonment. When tourists arrive to climb the mountain it will come alive again, serving as a welcome solid shelter from the cold daily rain of the summit.

As we hovered in the Melinau Gorge above Camp Five, figures appeared on the river bank waving: nomadic Penan returning to their old hunting grounds; a year before they would have remained hidden. From the air there was no trace of our activities; the helipads grassed over now, the well-marked trails invisible between the trees and the orange camp sheets removed and stored. Only at Base Camp were there signs of activity as we came in to land; a pile of boxes for collection, the last of our rubber boats and a group of Berawans waiting. Inggan, the strong one, now in charge, with tears streaming down his face as he greeted us. Unable to speak now that the final parting had come, he simply hugged us one by one.

I crossed the river in a longboat, climbing up the bank by the great log – the raft and steps had gone – to stand among the charred embers of our home for so long. With one of the RMAF crew who was a doctor I walked along the path to the little camp where we had heard that Seng, the old Penan headman, was lying sick. Two of his daughters were looking after him and the diagnosis was that all he needed was food and rest. Evacuating him to hospital would do no good.

For the first and only time I found myself beginning to wish in my heart that we had never started it all. The emptiness of leaving was overpowering; a feeling that we had achieved nothing for the people of Mulu, whatever we might have done for science, that we might even have done more harm than good; guilt at not having been able to reciprocate more fully the total welcome we had received from the start; gall and self-pity that all the golden days were over and we might never return.

We of the developed world will probably survive the problems being created by a shrinking planet and the resultant diminishing standards of living. So, too, will the farmers, fishermen and townspeople of the developing nations, although as the natural resources of their countries are plundered, so will their material expectations fail to materialize. The Berawans will survive, adapting and competing as changes come; their robust natures, strong sense of community and general desire to enter the modern world will see them through. But without the protecting canopy of their forests, the Penan will not. It is their life and their home. Adaptation will be slow and difficult at best, fatal at worst. Whatever happens to the forests, whether they are cut down for timber, taken over by scientists or developed for tourism, the Penan will be forced out in time. At least their forests are safe at present and the Penan are not alone. Good men care about their future and will help them through the difficult times ahead.

I felt I could not bear to say goodbye to Nyapun and his family, my dearest friends, and hoped they would not appear. As we came out into the main clearing by the river again I saw a close-knit group of men, women and children clustered round the big stump. Knowing it was them I turned away to take some photographs and hide my tears. With great dignity they waited solemn-faced until I was ready to embrace each, then walk to the bank without looking back. Little Anyi, laughing and crying at the same time, ran after me to catch my hand and force a last bead bracelet over my wrist.

As we took off the Berawans crouched under the wind of the rotor blades waving and shouting, their voices drowned by the din of the motor. Across the blue streak of the Melinau a row of slight figures carrying baskets and blowpipes trooped in single file out of the sunlight back into the cool shade of their forest home.

Afterword

Lord Shackleton

I FIRST saw Mulu when I looked at it through my theodolite from 4000 foot high Mount Dulit while taking bearings for a map of this part of Sarawak. I was a member of an Oxford University ecological expedition in 1932 based on the River Tinjar and organized by that remarkable man, Tom Harrisson.

It was early morning. Clouds lay in the valleys and there was a staggering view of the mountains of Central Borneo standing up through the mists. There was the needle spire of Batu Lawi, the twin peaks of Kalulong and, perhaps the most striking, the great mass of Mount Mulu.

We used to look out at Mulu over 70 miles away and wonder how we could reach it. Beyond it we could see the inaccessible Kelabit country into which Tom Harrisson was later to be dropped during the war to raise the inland people against the Japanese invaders. But at that time we had little thought that one day we should be able to enter those territories.

Mulu was to us something of a challenge, not very high by mountaineering standards, but allegedly unapproachable and unclimbable. It was said to be surrounded by swamps and precipices. The reality was even more striking – the huge limestone cliffs, the lofty rain forest with its thick canopy, and the friendliness and warmth of the people I travelled with.

In the last month Tom Harrisson decided that the expedition, having completed its main scientific work, should break up and that we would go our separate ways. Moore and Banks went to climb Mount Kalulong. The botanists and the entomologists pursued their particular courses, and Tom Harrisson, armed with a gramophone, went over the range of mountains behind the camp and down into the Rejang. He suggested that I should go off and try to climb Mount Mulu.

There is no need for me to attempt a description of this great mountain mass, for the whole of this remarkable book of Robin Hanbury-Tenison's gives as complete and splendid a picture as can be found of such a fascinating area. When I left the government station of Marudi in November, it was still something of a mystery. There had been a number of attempts by members of previous expeditions but the way had really only been found (as I discovered) by a rhinoceros hunter called Tama Nilong, who had followed a trail which led him past the cliffs until he reached the main south-west ridge of Mulu. He had a very difficult time, for he was without food for nearly thirteen days, but it was with him as guide, together with a party of nineteen other Berawans, that I set out. It was the rainy season and it had rained steadily for many days – a bad time anyway, for most of the people in the district were out planting rice. And there was the obstacle of the entertainment of the very hospitable people whose great desire in those days was always to have a party for any of the occasionally visiting scientists and district officers – not to mention the explorers. Luckily the flood went down and, when I set out from the empty wooden fort abandoned at Long Melinau on the Tutoh river, it was possible to travel only some way by boat towards the foot of the mountain.

The huge cliffs were very formidable, especially to someone who is by no means a rock climber. As we set out I remember walking past the spectacular perpendicular walls of Gunung Api, so reminiscent of Conan Doyle's *Lost World*. Occasionally we had glimpses of the whole of the Mulu range, for really it is a range rather than a single peak. Gunung Api, successfully climbed by Robin and his people, was to me a fascinating mountain. The limestone cliffs were apparently unscaleable and there were rumours of fires, perhaps caused by lightning. Indeed, there were some reports that it might have been volcanic; certainly there were hot springs in the neighbourhood.

The story of the first ascent of Mulu is perhaps no different from the stories of any other climbs on equatorial mountains. There was the endless march through the great virgin rain forest, attacked constantly by leeches. The climb was to take us seven days. The problem was to carry the heavy loads and, indeed, to persuade those intelligent people, the Berawans, that there was some point to climbing the mountain.

Although it was steep, the going during the first day or two was comparatively good, for the forest still consisted of big timber rising to a height of over one hundred feet. But it grew colder and soon we entered at around 4000 feet that extraordinary phenomenon, the moss forest. We were dependent, too, on trying to hunt, something which would be forbidden today, but we were able to get some pig and even some monkeys, which were popular with my companions. Sometimes we found ourselves plunging deeper and deeper, not knowing whether we were walking on the top of the wood or on the forest floor and occasionally having to cut tunnels through the squelching moss. Every tree was festooned with moss and its base was buried deep under the squelchy vegetation.

I remember the fifth day particularly well. The morning was lovely and clear as the sun fought down the mist – even the fantastic moss forest looked quite cheerful. A few hours of rapid marching brought us to the second peak at a height of 5800 feet. A wonderful view lay before us to the west and a bright sun made everything warm and pleasant. The usual rain set in, but it cleared later, and I sent most of the men out to collect plants and birds. We could see the path we had followed through the forest up to the south-western shoulder of Mulu and then along a semi-circular ridge connecting the first and second peaks. Pitcher plants and rhododendrons were abundant, and moss covered everything.

Towards evening it grew very cold and just before sunset the headman begged a little biscuit, whisky, butter, milk and two eggs with which to make the propitiatory sacrifice before completing the first ascent to the summit. Tama Nilong carried out the ceremony, which consisted of incantations murmured before some roughly carved bits of wood. A motley crowd in their borrowed pullovers and my shirts, the Berawans did not seem to take it very seriously and were far keener to help me take photographs before it grew too dark. The scene was one of the most bizarre and wonderful I have ever seen. The highest peak stood out black against the eastern sky, while to the west an exquisite sunset dissolved into a mixture of colours which is inconceivable to anyone who has never visited the tropics. To the west, fresh peaks stood out against the setting sun and nearly 6000 feet below us the river Tutoh glistened. That evening I hung out a couple of lamps as I had promised my friend the Penghulu, to show that we had reached the main ridge.

As we neared the peak on the seventh day we could see it through a tangled mass of brightly-coloured vegetation, with a crown of scarlet blossoming rhododendrons round the summit. The mountainside was covered with densely massed bushes and was a riot of red, yellow and green leaves, interspersed with flowers. To our joy, as we approached the peak, we saw no rock faces, though at points it was almost vertical. It was like climbing a tree. Soon the inevitable rain came on and the summit disappeared, but after a sheer climb we reached the summit and decided to camp there for the night. It seemed very cold after the warmth of the tropics, although the temperature was still over 50°F. But the men felt it greatly and the standard remark 'Sejok Tuan', meaning 'Cold, Sir', grew more frequent. The following morning, however, we had a wonderful view of the mountains standing out through the clouds. Then, looking over the dwarf trees, we saw yet another peak, higher still. I was anxious to get down with the men for we had used up all our food, but it seemed we could not resist this final challenge. Luckily the path we were able to cut was pretty easy and we reached the top of Mulu at 09.40 on 18 November 1932.

So, many years later, in the summer of 1978, it was marvellously exciting to return to Mount Mulu, to the jungle, the forests, those tremendous cliffs and, above all, the green mountains. Mulu was not a dramatic mountain in the sense of the great peaks Lord Hunt and the real mountaineers know, but it was filled with fascination for me – indeed, the final stages of my original ascent led by old Tama Nilong granted me some extraordinary mystical moments. It was, therefore, especially nostalgic to walk again through those deep forests with his grandson, Tama Bulan, as my guide – a magnificent young man, and the newly appointed warden of the Mulu National Park.

It was certainly Tom Harrisson's, as well as my own, hope that the Mulu area be made a national park. Indeed, we started a campaign advocating this many years ago, and I wrote an article to that effect for the Sarawak Museum Journal. Now it is a national park and I believe the work of Robin Hanbury-Tenison's expedition – perhaps the most successful expedition in scientific terms to be sent out by the Royal Geographical Society in modern times – will have contributed to the survival of a crucially valuable territory.

Fortunately there are some people, and even some governments, who now realize that it is essential to preserve forests not only to prevent erosion, flash floods, the silting up of rivers and other undesirable side effects, but also to preserve a source of genes which otherwise would be lost. We simply do not realize the significance of national parks for the conservation of wildlife and the rich variety of plants they contain. It is also sometimes possible to regenerate and recreate, and even significantly improve a damaged environment, but this calls for the most careful consideration and ecological understanding. In some circumstances and territories there is no recovery. It is virtually impossible to regenerate a self-balancing environment, as in the Kerangas Forest, to which Robin makes reference, once the trees have been cut down. The threat to our environment is not just from industry; it is notably, too, from agriculture and from logging, and the inexhaustible demand for the produce of woodlands. Even the move to draw on the biomass as a substitute source of energy will create dangers and difficulties.

At the present rate of disappearance of rain forests, it is estimated that one species becomes extinct every day and that within ten years the projected rate will be one every hour. Thus the danger of losing irreplaceable natural resources, the results of eons of evolution, is a very real one, while the elimination of natural predators, of both insects and plants, may lead to certain species reaching pest proportions.

The purpose of this expedition was, therefore, not just to pursue pure research in Mulu and to help develop a plan for the management of the National Park. In this sense alone the expedition was a great success, discovering a huge, still uncounted, number of new species and unravelling some of the complex questions posed by the richest environment on earth; but it also set out to influence authorities, both there and throughout the world, to adopt strong and consistant policies with regard to the preservation rather than the destruction of their forests. Conservation actually makes sound economic sense, as people like the Penan, who have come to terms with their environment, already know full well.

This is really what this book is about: it is about exploring and excitement and dedicated research, but there is also a message for the world.

Appendix A

BIRDS recorded within Gunung Mulu National Park compiled by Lord Cranbrook; list dated June 1979. The order of species follows Smythies, *Birds of Borneo*, 2nd edn., 1968.

Nomenclature has been updated to conform with present scientific conclusions.

PELECANIFORMES, the cormorants and allies

Anhinga melanogaster	Darter

ARDEIFORMES, the herons and storks

Butorides striatus	Little Green Heron
Goisakius melanolophus	Tiger Bittern
Ciconia stormi	Storm's Stork

FALCONIFORMES, the hawks and eagles

Macheiramphus alcinus	Bat Hawk
Pernis ptilorhyncus	Honey Buzzard
Haliastur indus	Brahminy Kite
Accipiter trivirgatus	Crested Goshawk
A. virgatus	Asiatic Sparrowhawk
Spizaetus alboniger	Blyth's Hawk Eagle
S. cf. nanus	(Wallace's) Hawk Eagle
Ictinaetus malayensis	Black Eagle
Icthyophaga humilis	Lesser Fish Eagle
Spilornis cheela	Crested Serpent Eagle
S. kinabaluensis	Kinabalu Serpent Eagle
Microhierax fringillarius	Black-thighed (Common) Falconet
Falco peregrinus	Peregrine Falcon

GALLIFORMES, the pheasants and partridges

Arborophila hyperythra	Red-breasted Tree Partridge
Melanoperdix nigra	Black Wood Partridge

Rollulus rouloul	Crested Green Wood Partridge
Haematortyx sanguiniceps	Crimson-headed Wood Partridge
Lophura erythrophthalma	Crestless Fireback Pheasant
L. ignita	Crested Fireback Pheasant
L. bulweri	Bulwer's Pheasant
Argusianus argus	Great Argus Pheasant

CHARADRIIFORMES, the gulls and waders

Actitis hypoleucos	Common Sandpiper

COLUMBIFORMES, the pigeons and doves

Treron capellei	Large Green Pigeon
T. curvirostra	Thick-billed Green Pigeon
Ptilinopus jambu	Jambu Fruit Pigeon
Ducula aenea	Green Imperial Pigeon
D. badia	Mountain Imperial Pigeon
Macropygia ruficeps	Little Cuckoo Dove
Chalcophaps indica	Emerald Dove

PSITTACIFORMES, the parrots

Loriculus galgulus	Malay Lorikeet

CUCLIFORMES, the cuckoos

Cuculus sparverioides	Large Hawk Cuckoo
C. fugax	Malayan Hawk Cuckoo
C. vagans	Moustached (Lesser) Hawk Cuckoo
C. micropterus	Indian Cuckoo
C. saturatus	Oriental Cuckoo
Cacomantis sonneratii	Banded Bay Cuckoo
C. variolosus	Fan-tailed Cuckoo
Surniculus lugubris	Drongo Cuckoo
Phaenicophaeus diardi	Lesser Green-billed Malcoha
P. chlorophaeus	Raffles' Malcoha
P. sumatranus	Rufous-bellied Malcoha
P. javanicus	Red-billed Malcoha
P. curvirostris	Chestnut-breasted Malcoha
Centropus sinensis	Common Coucal
C. rectunguis	Short-toed Coucal
Carpococcyx radiceus	Ground Cuckoo

STRIGIFORMES, the owls

Phodilus badius	Bay Owl
Otus rufescens	Reddish Scops Owl
O. spilocephalus	Mountain Scops Owl
O. ? brookei	(Rajah's) Scops Owl
Glaucidium brodiei	Pigmy Owlet
Ninox scutulata	Hawk Owl
Strix leptogrammica	Malaysian Wood Owl

CAPRIMULGIFORMES, the nightjars and allies

Batrachostomus auritus	Large Frogmouth
B. sp.	Frogmouth

APODIFORMES, the swifts

Aerodramus vanikorensis	Mossy-nest Swiftlet
A. fuciphagus	Edible-nest Swiftlet
Collocalia esculenta	White-bellied Swiftlet
Rhaphidura leucopygialis	White-rumped Spine-tail Swift
Hirundapus giganteus	Malaysian Spine-tailed Swift
Hemiprocne longipennis	Crested Tree-swift
H. comata	White-whiskered Tree-swift

TROGONIFORMES, the trogons

Harpactes diardi	Diard's Trogon
H. kasumba	Red-naped Trogon
H. whiteheadi	Whitehead's Trogon
H. duvauceli	Scarlet-rumped Trogon
H. orrhophaeus	Cinnamon-rumped Trogon
H. oresdias	Orange-breasted Trogon

CORACIIFORMES, the rollers and allies

Lacedo pulchella	Banded Kingfisher
Halcyon concreta	Chestnut-collared Kingfisher
H. pileata	Black-capped Kingfisher
Pelargopsis capensis	Stork-billed Kingfisher
Alcedo meninting	Deep Blue Kingfisher
A. euroyzona	Blue-banded Kingfisher
Ceyx erithacus (rufidorsus)	Forest Kingfisher
Nyctyotnis amictus	Red-bearded Bee-eater
Berenicornis comatus	White-crested Hornbill

Anorrhinus galeritus	Bushy-crested Hornbill
Rhyticeros corrugatus	Wrinkled Hornbill
R. undulatus	Wreathed Hornbill
Anthracoceros malayanus	Black Hornbill
A. coronatus	Pied Hornbill
Buceros rhinoceros	Rhinoceros Hornbill
Rhinoplax vigil	Helmet Hornbill

PICIFORMES, the woodpeckers and allies

Calorhamphus fuliginosus	Brown Barbet
Megalaima chrysopogon	Gold-whiskered Barbet
M. rafflesi	Many-coloured Barbet
M. mystacophanos	Gaudy Barbet
M. henricii	Yellow-crowned Barbet
M. pulcherrima	Golden-naped Barbet
M. monticola	Mountain Barbet
M. eximia	Black-throated Barbet
M. australis	Little Barbet
Sasia abnormis	Rufous Piculet
Picus puniceus	Crimson-winged Woodpecker
P. mentalis	Checker-throated Woodpecker
P. miniaceus	Banded Red Woodpecker
Celeus brachyurus	Rufous Woodpecker
Meiglyptes tristis	Fulvous-rumped Barred Woodpecker
M. tukki	Buff-necked Barred Woodpecker
Hemicircus concretus	Grey & Buff Woodpecker
Dinopium rafflesi	Olive-backed Three-toed Woodpecker
Muelleripicus pulverulentus	Great Slaty Woodpecker
Blythipicus rubiginosus	Maroon Woodpecker
Rheinwardtipicus validus	Orange-backed Woodpecker

PASSERES, the passerine birds

Calyptomena viridis	Green Broadbill
C. hosei	Hose's Broadbill
C. whiteheadi	Whitehead's Broadbill
Psarisomus dalhousiae	Long-tailed Broadbill
Cymbirhynchus macrorhynchos	Black and Red Broadbill
Eurylaimus ochromalus	Black and Yellow Broadbill

Eurylaimus javanicus	Banded Broadbill
Corydon sumatranus	Dusky Broadbill
Pitta arcuata	Blue-banded Pitta
P. granatina	Garnet Pitta
P. baudi	Blue-headed Pitta
Hirundo tahitica	Pacific Swallow
H. rustica	Barn Swallow
Motacilla caspica	Grey Wagtail
M. flava	Yellow Wagtail
Tephrodornis gularis	Hook-billed Greybird
Coracina larvata	Black-faced Greybird
C. fimbriata	Lesser Greybird
Hemipus hirundinaceus	Black-winged Flycatcher-Strike
H. picatus	Bar-winged Flycatcher-Strike
Chlamydochaera jeffreyi	Black-breasted Triller
Pericrocotus solaris	Mountain Minivet
P. flammeus	Scarlet Minivet
Aegithina viridissima	Green Iora
Chloropsis cyanopogon	Lesser Green Leafbird
C. sonnerati	Greater Green Leafbird
C. cochinchinensis	Blue-winged Leafbird
Irena puella	Fairy Bluebird
Pycnonotus eutilotus	Crested Brown Bulbul
P. melanoleucos	Black and White Bulbul
P. atriceps	Black-headed Bulbul
P. squamatus	Scaly-breasted Bulbul
P. cyaniventris	Grey-bellied Bulbul
P. zeylanicus	Yellow-crowned Bulbul
P. flavescens	Pale-faced Bulbul
P. plumosus	Large Olive Bulbul
P. brunneus	Red-eyed Brown Bulbul
P. simplex	Cream-vented (White-eyed) Brown Bulbul
P. erythropthalmus	Lesser Brown Bulbul
Criniger bres	Scrub (Olive White-throated) Bulbul
C. ochraceus	Brown White-throated Bulbul
C. phaeocephalus	Crestless White-throated Bulbul
C. finschii	Finsch's Bulbul

Setornis criniger	Hook-billed Bulbul
Hypsipetes criniger	Hairy-backed Bulbul
H. malaccensis	Streaked Bulbul
H. charlottae	Crested Olive Bulbul
H. flavala	Ashy Bulbul
Erithacus cyane	Siberian Blue Robin
Brachypteryx montana	Blue Shortwing
Copsychus pyrropyga	Orange-tailed Shama
C. saularis	Magpie Robin
C. malabaricus	White-rumped Shama
Enicurus leschenaulti	White-crowned Forktail
E. ruficapillus	Chestnut-naped Forktail
Zoothera everettii	Everett's Ground Thrush
Myophoneus glaucinus	Sunda Whistling Thrush
Eupetes macrocerus	Rail Babbler
Pellorneum capistratum	Black-capped Jungle Babbler
Trichastoma pyrrhogenys	Temmick's Jungle Babbler
T. malaccense	Short-tailed Jungle Babbler
T. rostratum	Blyth's Jungle Babbler
T. bicolor	Ferruginous Jungle Babbler
T. sepiarium	Horsfield's Jungle Babbler
Malacopteron magnum	Greater Red-headed Tree Babbler
M. cinereum	Lesser Red-headed Tree Babbler
M. magnirostre	Moustached Babbler
M. albogulare	White-throated Babbler
Pomatorhinus montanus	Chestnut-backed Scimitar Babbler
Ptilocichla leucogrammica	Bornean Wren Babbler
Kenopia striata	Striped Wren Babbler
Napothera atrigularis	Black-throated Wren Babbler
N. crassa	Mountain Wren Babbler
N. epilepidota	Small Wren Babbler
Macronus ptilosus	Fluffy-backed Tit Babbler
Stachyris nigriceps	Grey-throated Tree Babbler
S. poliocephala	Grey-headed Tree Babbler
S. nigricollis	Black-necked Tree Babbler
S. leucotis	White-necked Tree Babbler
S. maculata	Red-rumped Tree Babbler
S. erythroptera	Red-winged Tree Babbler
S. rufifrons	Hume's Tree Babbler

Garrulax lugubris	Black Laughing Thrush
G. palliatus	Grey & Brown Laughing Thrush
G. mitratus	Chestnut-capped Laughing Thrush
Pteruthius flaviscapis	Red-winged Shrike Babbler
Alcippe brunneicauda	Brown Quaker Babbler
Minla castaneiceps	Chestnut-headed Minla
Yuhina zantholeuca	White-bellied Yuhina
Gerygone sulphurea	Flyeater
Cettia whiteheadi	Short-tailed Bush Warbler
C. fortipes	Mountain Bush Warbler
Phylloscopus borealis	Arctic Leaf Warbler
P. trivirgatus	Mountain Leaf Warbler
Seicercus montis	Yellow-breasted Flycatcher Warbler
Abroscopus superciliaris	White-throated Flycatcher Warbler
Orthotomus cuculatus	Mountain Tailorbird
O. ruficeps	Ashy (Red-headed) Tailorbird
Rhipidura albicollis	White-throated Fantail Flycatcher
R. perlata	Spotted Fantail Flycatcher
R. javanica	Pied Fantail Flycatcher
Culicicapa ceylonensis	Grey-headed Flycatcher
Muscicapa sibirica	Sooty Flycatcher
M. latirostris	Brown Flycatcher
M. indigo	Indigo Flycatcher
Cyanoptila cyanomelana	Blue and White Flycatcher
Cyornis concreta	White-tailed Blue Flycatcher
C. unicolor	Pale Blue Flycatcher
C. turcosa	Malaysian Blue Flycatcher
C. caerulata	Large-billed Blue Flycatcher
C. banyumas	Hill Blue Flycatcher
C. superba	Bornean Blue Flycatcher
Ficedula hyperythra	White-fronted Blue Flycatcher
F. dumetoria	Orange-breasted Flycatcher
F. westermanni	Little Pied Flycatcher
Muscicapella hodgsoni	Pigmy Blue Flycatcher
Rhinomyias umbratilis	White-throated Jungle Flycatcher
R. ruficauda	Rufous-tailed Jungle Flycatcher
R. gularis	White-browed Jungle Flycatcher
Philentoma pyrhoterum	Chestnut-winged Monarch Flycatcher

P. velatum	Maroon-breasted Monarch Flycatcher
Hypothymis azurea	Black-naped Blue Monarch Flycatcher
Terpsiphone paradisi	Paradise Flycatcher
Pachycephala hypoxantha	Bornean Mountain Whistler
Sitta frontalis	Velvet-fronted Nuthatch
Prionochilus thoracicus	Scarlet-breasted Flowerpecker
P. xanthopygius	Yellow-rumped Flowerpecker
P. maculatus	Yellow-throated Flowerpecker
Dicaeum chrysorrheum	Yellow-vented Flowerpecker
D. monticola	Black-sided Flowerpecker
Anthreptes simplex	Plain-coloured Sunbird
A. rhodolaema	Rufous-throated Sunbird
A. singalensis	Ruby-cheeked Sunbird
Hypogramma hypogrammicum	Purple-naped Sunbird
Aethopyga siparaja	Yellow-backed Sunbird
A. mystacalis	Scarlet Sunbird
Arachnothera longirostra	Little Spiderhunter
A. robusta	Long-billed Spiderhunter
A. affinis	Grey-breasted Spiderhunter
A. juliae	Whitehead's Spiderhunter
Zosterops atricapilla	Black-capped White-eye
Chlorocharis emiliae	Mountain Blackeye
Gracula religiosa	Grackle or Talking Myna
Erythrura hyperythra	Bamboo Munia
Dicrurus annectans	Crow-billed Drongo
D. leucophaeus	Grey Drongo
D. hottentottus	Hair-crested Drongo
D. paradiseus	Large Racket-tailed Drongo
Oriolus xanthonotus	Black-headed Oriole
O. cruentus	Black and Crimson Oriole
Platylophus galericulatus	Crested Jay
Dendrocitta occipitalis	Malaysian Treepie
Crovus enca	Slender-billed Crow

262 species

Appendix B

MAMMALS recorded within Gunung Mulu National Park, collated by the Earl of Cranbrook, June 1979; records from expedition Base Camp, Long Pala (outside Park boundary) are excluded.

The order of species follows Medway, *Mammals of Borneo*, Monogr., Malaysian Branch Royal Asiatic Society, No. 7, 1978.

INSECTIVORA, the insectivores

Echinosorex gymnurus	Moon rat
Hylomys suillus	Lesser Gymnure
Suncus etruscus	Savi's Pigmy Shrew
Crocidura monticola	Sunda Shrew
Tupaia montana	Mountain Tree Shrew
T. picta	Painted Tree Shrew
Dendrogale melanura	Smooth-tailed Tree Shrew

DERMOPTERA, the colugos

Cynocephalus variegatus	Flying Lemur

CHIROPTERA, the bats

Pteropus vampyrus	Flying Fox
Cyanopterus branchyotis	Malaysian Fruit Bat
Balionycteris maculata	Spotted-winged Fruit Bat
Aethalops alecto	Grey Fruit Bat
Penthetor lucasii	Dusky Fruit Bat
Rhinolophus borneensis	Borneo Horseshoe Bat
R. creaghi	Creagh's Horseshoe Bat
R. philippensis	Philippine Horseshoe Bat
Coelops robinsoni	Lesser Tailless Horseshoe Bat
Hipposideros galeritus	Cantor's Roundleaf Horseshoe Bat
H. insolens	Lyon's Roundleaf Horseshoe Bat
H. diadema	Diadem Roundleaf Horseshoe Bat

Myotis horsfieldii	Horsfield's Bat
Philetor brachypterus	Short-winged Brown Bat
Murina cyclotis	Round-eared Tube-nosed Bat
Tadarida plicata	Wrinkled-lipped Bat

PRIMATES, the monkeys, apes and relatives

Tarsius bancanus	Western Tarsier
Presbytis hosei	Grey Leaf Monkey
P. rubicunda	Maroon Leaf Monkey
P. cristata	Silvered Leaf Monkey
Macaca fascicularis	Long-tailed Macaque
M. nemestrina	Pig-tailed Macaque
Hylobates muelleri	Bornean Gibbon
Nycticebus coucang	Slow Loris

RODENTIA, the rodents

Ratufa affinis	Giant Squirrel
Callosciurus prevostii	Prevost's Squirrel
C. baluensis	Kinabalu Squirrel
C. notatus	Plantain Squirrel
Sundasciurus hippurus	Horse-tailed Squirrel
S. jentinki	Jentink's Squirrel
Lariscus insignis	Three-striped Ground Squirrel
Dremomys everetti	Bornean Mountain Ground Squirrel
Exilisciurus exilis	Plain Pigmy Squirrel
E. whiteheadi	Whitehead's Pigmy Squirrel
Rheithrosciurus macrotis	Tufted Ground Squirrel
Aeromys tephromelas	Black Giant Flying Squirrel
Rattus muelleri	Müller's Rat
R. infraluteus	Mountain Giant Rat
R. cremoriventer	Dark-tailed Tree Rat
R. surifer	Red Spiny Rat
R. whiteheadi	Whitehead's Rat
R. rapit	Mountain Long-tailed Rat
R. sabanus	Long-tailed Giant Rat
Chiropodomys gliroides	Tree-mouse (unidentified)
Trichys lipura	Long-tailed Porcupine
Hysterix/Thecurus	Large porcupines (not positively identified)

Carnivora, the carnivores

Helarctos malayanus	Sun Bear
Martes flavigula	Yellow-throated Marten
Lutra sp./Amblonyx	Otters (not positively identified)
Viverra tangalunga	Malay Civet
Paradoxurus hermaphroditus	Common Palm Civet
Arctictis binturong	Bearcat
Arctogalidia trivirgata	Three-striped Palm Civet
Hemigalus derbyanus	Banded Palm Civet
Herpestes sp.	Mongoose

Artiodactyla, the cloven-hoofed ungulates

Sus barbatus	Bearded Pig
Tragulus sp., cf. javanicus	(Lesser) Mouse-deer
Muntiacus muntjak	Barking Deer
Cervus unicolor	Sambur

67 species

Appendix C

Leader and Field Director: Robin Hanbury-Tenison

Deputy Field Director: Nigel de N. Winser

Secretariat: Sandy Evans, Shane Wesley-Smith

Field Support: Amy Herbert, Hamdan bin Abang Jawi, Philip Leworthy, Ricky Nelson, Michael Pengiran Sia, Abdul Manaf Sairi, Peter Wedlake, Margriet Maurenbrecher, Robert Jamal Yapik, Yau Kwok Wai

Catering: Kate Clark, Rosemary Fullerton-Smith, Marika Hanbury Tenison, Wilma Lloyd-Smith, Rosie Sadler, Uschi Trosch

Medical Team: Constance Dennehy, David Giles, Nicola Ingram, Gerry Mitton, John Ogle, Ivan Polunin, Paul Sepping, Alan Lloyd-Smith

Scientific Programme Co-ordinator: Clive Jermy

Scientific projects investigated by members of the Royal Geographical Society/Sarawak Government Expedition to Gunung Mulu 1977–8:

Botanical

1. To study the ecology and delimit and map the forest formations of the Park (J.A.R. Anderson, P.C. Chai and Sarawak Forest Department Team)

2. Ecological studies on nutrient balance and flow in four forest types (J.M. Anderson, N.M. Collins, S. Leche, J. Proctor, S.C. Proctor, H. Vallack)

3. A taxonomic and ecological study of flowering plant families, particularly the following:
    (a) Rhododendrons (*Ericaceae*) (G. Argent, J.A.R. Kerby)
    (b) Mimosa family (*Leguminosae*) (S. Lewis, I.C. Nielsen)
    (c) Spider Flower Family (*Melastomataceae*) (C.K. Hansen)
    (d) Palms (*Palmaceae*) (J. Dransfield, T.C. Whitmore)
    (e) Screw-pines (*Pandanaceae*) (B.C. Stone)
4. A study of the distribution of the wild sago (J. Dransfield, C.K. Hansen, A.C. Jermy, I.C. Nielsen, T.C. Whitmore)

5. An ecological study of the herbaceous plants of the forest floor (R. Kiew)

6. Taxonomic, ecological and chromosome survey of ferns (*Pteridophyta*) (B.S. Croxall, J. Croxall, A.C. Jermy, T.G. Walker)

7. Taxonomic and ecological survey of mosses and liverworts (A. Touw)

8. Taxonomic and ecological survey of fungi (B. Coppins, W.F.B. Julich)

9. Taxonomic and ecological survey of lichens (B. Coppins, N. Sammy)

Zoological

1. The distribution of the mammals in the different forest types (Lord Cranbrook, D. Labang, P.M.H. Leworthy, A.W. Mitchell)

2. Radio tagging and behaviour studies of selected mammals (D. Macdonald, M. Wise)

3. The diversity and abundance of birds in relation to vegetation changes (J. Croxall, G.W.H. Davison, C.J. & S.A. Hails, K. McCormick, B. Sage, D.R. Wells)

4. The calls of lowland and montane birds (B. King)

5. The distribution, breeding behaviour and vocal diversity of frogs and toads (J.C. Dring, B.H. Kiew)

6. Resource studies in selected lizard species (I.R. Swingland)

7. The distribution and taxonomy of fish (J. Cramphorn)

8. The physical and chemical environment of selected rivers (B.H. Kiew, K.S. Liew, R.P. Lim)

9. The collection of vertebrate blood samples for parasite content (W. Peters, C.M. Saunders)

10. Collection and ecological studies on cave faunas (P. Chapman, S.C. Proctor)

11. The collection, taxonomy and ecology of selected insect groups, in particular the following:
    (a) Ants (*Hymenoptera: Formicidae*) (B. Bolton)
    (b) Aphids (*Hemiptera: Homoptera*) (V.F. Eastop)
    (c) Bugs (*Hemiptera*) and short-horned grasshoppers (*Orthoptera: Acridoidea*) (D. Hollis)
    (d) Beetles (*Coleoptera* especially *Staphylinidae*) including larval stages (P.M. Hammond, J.E. Marshall)

12. The role of termites in the ecology and decomposition of different rain forest formations (N.M. Collins)

13. The distribution and diversity of beetles (*Coleoptera*) in relation to forest type and altitude (P.M. Hammond, I. Hanski)

14. Comparative studies of butterflies and moths (*Lepidoptera*) in relation to forest type and altitude (J.D. Holloway)

15. A study of mimicry in the butterfly family *Danaidae* (A.L. Panchen)

16. The distribution and taxonomy of spiders (*Arachnida*) (F.R. Wanless)

17. The distribution and ecology of centipedes and millipedes (*Myriapoda*) (J.C. Lewis)

Geomorphology

1. A study of the rates of erosion and formation of land forms (M.J. Day, R. Day, M. Sweeting, R.P.D. Walsh)

2. Climatological observations (S.C. Proctor, R.P.D. Walsh)

3. The geomorphology of the Quaternary terraces (C. Woodroffe)

4. A survey of the soils of the Park (I. Baillie, C.P. Lim, C. Phang, Y.L. Tie)

5. The hydrology and chemistry of the limestone (H. Friederich)

6. Limestone dissolution dynamics and karst micro-morphology.(D.L. Dunkerley)

7. A study of the limestone towers and pinnacles (R. Ley, R. McDonald)

8. Erosion rates and karren studies (H. A. Osmaston, N. Osmaston)

9. Micro-palaeontology and magnetostratographical studies (T. Ooi, K. T. Yap)

10. A topographical and geomorphological survey of the cave systems (D. Brook, A.J. Eavis, M. Farnworth, M.K. Lyon, A.C. Waltham)

11. Cave clay sediment studies and chemical composition of ground waters (M. Laverty)

Ethnology

1. A study of the movements and diet of the Punans and an assessment of their ecological status within the Park ecosystem (A.J.U. Anderson, P.M. Kedit and the Sarawak Museum Team)

Bibliography

BROOK, D. B., and WALTHAM, A. C., *Caves of Mulu*, Royal Geographical Society, London, 1978.

COLLINS, N. M., 'In Wallace's Footsteps: Entomologists at the Gunong Mulu National Park, Sarawak', *Antenna*, No. 3, 1979.

HANBURY-TENISON, R., 'Virgin Rainforest of Sarawak', *Geographical Magazine*, 50, 1977.

'Operation Rain Forest', *Illustrated London News*, 267 (6966), 1978.

HARRISSON, T., 'The Oxford University Expedition to Sarawak, 1932, *Geographical Journal*, 82, 1933.

HOSE, C., *The Field-Book of a Jungle-Wallah*, Whiterby, London, 1929.

INGER, R. F., 'The Systematics and Zoogeography of the Amphibia of Borneo', *Fieldiana: Zoology*, 52, 1966.

KING, B. F., and DICKINSON, E. C., *Birds of South-East Asia*, Collins, London, 1975.

LOW, H., *Sarawak*, Richard Bentley, London, 1848.

MEDWAY, LORD, 'Mammals of Borneo', Field list and annotated checklist, J. Malaysian Branch Royal Asiatic Society 36(3), No. 203, 1965.

Second edition, 1977, Monograph Malaysian Branch of Royal Asiatic Society, No. 7.

MACKINNON, J., et al, *Borneo*, Time-Life, Amsterdam.

SMYTHIES, B., *Birds of Borneo*, 2nd ed., Oliver & Boyd, London, 1968.

ST JOHN, S., *Life in the Forests of the Far East; or Travels in Northern Borneo*, vols 1 & 2, Smith, Elder, London, 1862.

SWEETING, M., 'It Always Rains in Gunung Mulu, *Geographical Magazine*, 51, 1979.

WALLACE, A. R., *The Malay Archipelago*, Macmillan, 1898.

WILFORD, G. E., 'The Geology and Mineral Resources of Brunei and Adjacent Parts of Sarawak', Mem. Geol. Surv. Dept. Brit. Borneo, 10, 1961.

WINSER, N DE N, 'Mulu: Invitation to a Tropical Rain Forest', Expedition Magazine, Wexas, London, 1979.

WHITMORE, T. C., *Tropical Rain Forests of the Far East*, Clarendon Press, Oxford, 1975.

Index

KING ALFRED'S COLLEGE
LIBRARY